The Master Musicians

New Series Revised and Edited by Eric Blom, C.B.E., D.Litt.

RAVEL

Gordon Bryan

Maurice Ravel

The Master Musicians

RAVEL

by

NORMAN DEMUTH

Illustrated

London   J. M. Dent and Sons Ltd
New York   Farrar, Straus and Cudahy Inc.

D 381/2 m

FOREWORD

THE sources of information for the biographical section of this, the first book on Ravel by an English author, are *A la Gloire de Ravel* (Roland-Manuel), published in 1938 by *Nouvelle Revue critique*, *Maurice Ravel* (by some of his friends), published by the Éditions de Tambourinaire in 1939, and the special number of *La Revue musicale* devoted entirely to the composer, issued in December 1938.

One other authority is a 'Biographical Sketch' which the composer prepared for a firm of player-piano manufacturers who commissioned certain composers to write works specially for their instruments. Ravel was always averse to writing and talking about himself, but M. Roland-Manuel, one of his most faithful pupils and friends, conceived the idea of jotting down the details which Ravel gave him verbally and setting them up in tabulated form. This 'Biographical Sketch' was printed for the first time in the special number of *La Revue musicale*.

Grove's Dictionary and other similar works have been combed for information on various names of importance in France, but unknown in this country. It is regretted that all these volumes omit reference to many whose position in their own land seems to warrant consideration.

I wish to thank Messrs. J. & W. Chester Ltd. and the United Music Publishers Ltd. for their unstinted loan of music, also the various performers who have so kindly contributed their own personal opinions of and reactions to works by Ravel which they have played, thus adding very considerably to the interest of the book.

I am very grateful to Mr. Gordon Bryan for the use of the photographs taken by himself, to MM. Durand et Cie, Paris, for the photograph of Ravel taken in 1914, and to M. Robert Bernard, editor of *La Revue musicale*, for the use of the blocks of the photographs which appeared in the 1938 special Ravel number of that journal.

The following have kindly consented to the use of quotations from works of which they are the publishers: MM. Rouart, Lerolle et Cie, Paris, *Trois Sarabandes* (Erik Satie); MM. Enoch et fils, Paris, *Menuet antique* (American copyright: 1898); Messrs. Schott & Co., London, and Max Eschig, Paris, *Pavane pour une Infante défunte, Jeux d'eau, Miroirs*; MM. Durand et Cie, Paris, for the remainder.

Finally, I would like to thank Mr. J. A. Sowerbutts and Mr. Felix Aprahamian for so kindly reading the proofs in their several stages.

N. D.

Bognor Regis,
May 1946.

CONTENTS

ILLUSTRATIONS

CHAPTER I

WE find the family name mentioned for the first time in the birth and death registers at Collonges-sous-Salévé, a village in Haute-Savoie. There it is spelt Ravex and Ravet. The composer's grandfather, Aimé (or Ami), was born in 1800, and the name was entered as Ravex. When his great-grandfather, François, died in 1804 the name was entered in the register as Ravet. Ravex, Ravet and Ravez are all Savoyard surnames and the pronunciation is the same in each case. It is considered that the determination of the name as Ravel was due to a misreading of the final 't' in Ravet. However, the final form is by no means uncommon. There is a place in Puy-de-Dôme called Ravel-Salmerange, while in the middle of the nineteenth century there lived in Paris a popular comedian named Pierre Alfred Ravel.

It is also a Jewish surname, becoming in this case Rabbele. For this reason, and for the fact that Maurice Ravel not only included many Jews among his closest friends, but harmonized certain Hebrew melodies, his detractors have often accused him of Semitic origin. Truly no stick is bad enough! It has been confirmed that there was no trace of Jewish blood in his family.

Of the great-grandfather nothing is known. The grandfather was a baker at Versoix. In 1832 he had a son, Joseph, by his wife, formerly Caroline Grosfort, and in 1834 became a naturalized Swiss.

In 1868 Joseph Ravel was living at Neuilly, near Paris. He was a civil engineer with inventive tendencies. He was known as 'the man who made the first petrol carriage go.'[1] In January of that year he received a licence for his vehicle to proceed along the public highway, escorted by two policemen on foot. The first journey was not without incident. The weather was

[1] *Maurice Ravel*, by Some of his Friends.

intensely cold and Joseph had frequently to warm his escort up with glasses of rum and grog at various hostelries. The result was that the escort was incapable of doing very much escorting, and Joseph arrived at Saint-Denis in two hours, a veritable triumph.

Joseph had a brother, Édouard, who was a well-known interior decorative artist. With his own creative faculty and the artistic background of his brother, of whom he saw a great deal, Joseph had the attributes of a sympathetic father to any children with creative or productive leanings he might have.

After the Franco-Prussian war of 1870-1, Joseph Ravel went to Spain on business. In 1874 he married Marie Delouart who lived in New Castile. On 7th March 1875 she gave birth to Maurice Ravel at 12 Quai de la Nivelle, Ciboure, a sea-port on the Basque coast separating Nivelle from Saint-Jean-de-Luz. Thus the basis of so many of the future composer's thoughts was established from the very first, and it will be important to remember this all through our study.

At the age of seven Maurice began to take piano lessons from Henri Ghys. This worthy enthusiast, devoted to children, kept a log-book of his pupils, and on 31st May 1882 he made a note of the fact that his little pupil Maurice Ravel 'seemed intelligent.'

From the 'Biographical Sketch' [1] we learn that Ravel was 'aware of music of all kinds.' He was instinctive and very soon gave evidence of it. At the age of twelve he studied harmony with Charles René. This teacher believed in making all his students regard their exercises in the light of composition. This was a remarkably enlightened outlook for the period, and it is useful to remember that this principle is the guiding one of teachers like Paul Hindemith to-day. René was a disciple of Léo Delibes, the famous composer of ballets. Ravel wrote some Variations on a Chorale by Schumann which so astonished Réné by their originality that twenty-five years later he was still amazed at them.

[1] See Foreword.

The year 1887 is described by M. Roland-Manuel [1] as 'a great year for French music.' Certainly it heralded the dawn of a period propitious for any music student with latent originality, with a bent for enterprise and experiment, who needed but slight encouragement to kick over the traces. Debussy had begun the composition of *La Damoiselle élue* in Rome and Erik Satie had startled his friends with the individuality of his *Sarabandes* for piano in which he 'did things' no one else had either thought of or dared to do. It must be remembered that Ravel was completely outside the musical activities of Paris, being so young, and this proves his early style to have been perfectly natural, instinctive and individual.

In 1889 he was admitted to the preparatory piano class at the Conservatoire. Paris was occupied with the famous Exposition Universelle in the Rue de Caire. Through this exhibition passed every culture in the world—the French have always shown a flair for these things—and Maurice Ravel was a constant visitor. There he received a revelation. For the first time one could study orientalism first-hand, and Ravel fell under the sway of oriental scales and rhythms, together with the *bibelots* and other tokens of eastern culture which were exhibited there. Here was laid the foundation for the taste in things decorative which remained with him all his life.

In 1891 he was sufficiently advanced to enter the piano class of Charles de Bériot, the son of the violinist. In this class he made one of those fast friendships which are so common to youth and so valuable for any creative artist. Ricardo Viñes was exactly the same age as Ravel and, better still, had Catalan blood which was in sympathy with Ravel's Basque element. The result was that Viñes played everything Ravel composed, and we may well hazard a guess at the usefulness of the experiments which the two carried out together. Ravel found himself, therefore, in his natural world, and this was enhanced by the fact that Bériot had had connections with García and Malibran.

[1] *A la Gloire de Ravel*, 1938.

Bériot was not satisfied with Ravel as a pupil. Ricardo Viñes, with Robert Bernard as mouthpiece, says [1] that Bériot told Ravel that he was

a criminal; instead of being at the top of his class, he was at the bottom. In order to conquer his dislike of practising the piano, his mother conceived the idea of giving him six sous for every hour's work—the wages of a housemaid in those days. The scheme would have worked with any one else but Ravel, and if he had not had a balcony and so many reasons—Place Pigalle!—for running out every five minutes under the pretence or excuse that there had been an accident, a passing fire-engine, a street row or a bird which had flown into a neighbouring trap—and then he had music itself—and all those hitherto unthought of resolutions, those voluptuous dissonances, those polyphonic games which were able to give so much more relish than tiring five-finger exercises, and all those problems, fascinating and hazardous, which occupied Ravel's imagination so much more than the sporting interest of working the fourth finger.

He was by no means a docile student. It was not in his constitution to take things as they came or to bow to authority simply because it was authority. Like the perfect rebel, he took a fiendish delight in showing his professors music which he knew they would not like and noting each one's reactions—doubtless passing on each opinion in turn. Cynicism of any kind is never advisable in an institution unless the victims are known to be sufficiently receptive to take things in the right spirit—and it is to be feared that Ravel's own spirit was rarely the right one.

The professors who suffered so much at the hands of the rebel were men of eminence in their day. Émile Pessard won the Prix de Rome in 1866. He was a prolific writer of light operas much admired by Debussy. Napoléon Henri Reber was another dramatic composer. His chief mission was to free French music from the noise and bombast which had become fashionable. Théodore Dubois was primarily an organist, but he wrote much dramatic as well as church music. Organists still play his

[1] *La Revue musicale*, December 1938.

Hosannah (*Chorus Magnus*). He was head of the Conservatoire from 1886 to 1905, resigning as a result of a scandal regarding the Prix de Rome, which will be dealt with in the next chapter.

These were the men who tried to tame the original mind of Maurice Ravel, and hard put to it they were to control his impertinences.

Among the works with which Ravel enlivened the hunting down of fifths and octaves and brought grey hairs to the heads of his teachers were the *Chanson pour Jean* by Chabrier and the unpublished *Sarabandes* by Erik Satie. He and Viñes, with all the enthusiasm of youth, played Chabrier's *Trois Valses romantiques* to their composer, who was much entertained by this homage and gave both much encouragement. Chabrier was a sad figure. At the end of his life he was afflicted with a brain disease which forbade his recognizing his own music.

Ravel's admiration for Satie was unbounded, and he maintained to his dying day that he owed a great debt to him. This lonely figure was so far ahead of his time that instead of catching up with the latest ideas, he had the unique experience of seeing them 'catch up with him.' [1] He was a quaint figure, always wanting to be taken seriously, but never fortunate enough to be so taken outside his own immediate circle. Ravel's attitude had a serious repercussion some years later. One cannot envisage anything like this happening to-day.

As regards the older composers the first in Ravel's affections was Schumann, followed by Weber, Chopin and Liszt. It is noteworthy that three of these were essentially composers for the piano, and it will be seen that the last influenced him to an inordinate degree.

A composer, no matter how great he may become, will always regard his first composition as a landmark in his life. The sight of one's first published composition is an experience which can never be repeated, or forgotten. This is common to all: Dickens recorded that when his first published article appeared, he paced

[1] Constant Lambert, *Music Ho!*

up and down Westminster Hall, reading it over and over again and bursting with pride. This great thrill is unique and the composer re-lives it constantly, even though he may smile at the 'masterpiece' in his maturity. Ravel's first published work appeared in 1895, a *Menuet antique* for piano. This piece is remarkable for its prophecies of the future. Its free use of sevenths and ninths regardless of their resolutions gives us the foundations of that elegance and polish which became his greatest characteristic.

In the same year he composed the first of two pieces for two pianos, known collectively as *Les Sites auriculaires*. This was the *Habanera* which he was to use years later in its original state in the *Rapsodie espagnole*.

CHAPTER II

AT the age of twenty Ravel's mind was settled along its own definite lines. Adventurous in music, he was equally so in literature—Poe, Baudelaire, Mallarmé were among his 'discoveries,' discoveries which were not limited to the poetry but included the aesthetic treatises. In particular Poe's views of the origin of a poem and Baudelaire's on romantic art led to an interest in philosophy, and he read with avidity Condillac's *Treatise on Sensations* and Diderot's *Paradox of the Comedian*. This love of literature was with him all his life, but he was curiously reticent about it. No books were ever seen on his shelves, and it seemed as if he regarded his literary loves as a jealously guarded and personal secret which could be shared with nobody.

Musically things were growing increasingly exciting. Debussy's *Prélude à l'Après-midi d'un faune* had appeared in 1894 and had transported Ravel to new worlds, although it had passed almost unnoticed. Its sensuous sound and dreamy passion opened up fresh vistas to the disposal of the young student and these led him far away from Pessard and Dubois. He became friendly with Debussy and many years later made, as a labour of homage, an arrangement for two pianos of the *Prélude*. The Russians were just beginning to get out of Russia, and although the propaganda was slow and the knowledge was confined to Borodin and Rimsky-Korsakov, they left their mark, especially the latter, whose influence on Ravel in the matter of orchestration was immense.

The situation in other countries was not so promising. In England things were at the beginning of what is known as the 'Renaissance of British Music.' Parry had produced *Prometheus Unbound* in 1880 and *Blest Pair of Sirens* in 1887, and was all set for the non-stop production of festival works which make such depressing study. Elgar had got as far as *King Olaf* in 1896—

the 'Enigma' Variations had not yet been composed. Generally speaking, we were under the tyranny of the cathedral organists and the influence of Brahms. In Germany Brahms was to die two years later and Strauss was to be the high-light. In Russia Skriabin was twenty-four years old and not giving many signs of what was to follow.

There was no country producing music as advanced as that of France. Dukas was to bring out *L'Apprenti sorcier* in 1897, having in 1896 composed his Symphony and piano Sonata. Roussel was at the beginning of his career. Of the older composers Saint-Saëns was considered the leader, while a new man was coming along with a flair for Wagner—Vincent d'Indy. The great ruffler of the placid waters of musical France was, indeed, Wagner, and his influence was beginning to disturb those who, being Frenchmen and having a different outlook, could not bow the knee to Baal but preferred a Baal-type of their own. Thus other countries were proceeding along traditional lines, smug in the sense of their insularity and knowledge of what was music and what was not, while in France things were beginning to simmer.

In 1896 Ravel set Mallarmé's *Sainte* (which was published) and added *Entre Cloches* to the *Habanera* for two pianos, completing the work known as *Les Sites auriculaires*. *Entre Cloches* was not published and is unknown. This may not seem a great output for a young man of twenty-one, judged by the perfervid speed with which young composers to-day rush into ink and print; but Ravel had learned the art of self-criticism and had acquired that virtue of fastidiousness which remained a characteristic all his life.

The following year saw his promotion to the composition class of Gabriel Fauré, who had succeeded Massenet. This perfect *maître* and exquisite composer was the urge and inspiration of every young composer. With Fauré for composition and André Gédalge for counterpoint, Ravel had two teachers of whom he never spoke but in terms of the highest reverence.

We hear a lot about the difficulties that composers come up

8

against when they try to get a work performed. It may still be difficult, but Ravel had to wait until he was twenty-three before he had his first experience with the public. On 5th March 1898 Marthe Dron and Ricardo Viñes gave the first performance of *Les Sites auriculaires*. It would seem that the players did not fully control the resonances and sonorities, and the audience received the work with audible disapproval: this was not to be the last time that Ravel's music was to stir its hearers to anger. If we consider the sort of music to which audiences were wont to listen, and then think of the *Habanera* as we know it to-day (which, except for the orchestral transcription, is exactly as it stood then), we can see the reason for its failure. Audiences wanted a tune and not experiments in local colour and sonorities.

Ravel was not drawn into the Wagnerian vortex. Not for him the pomps and vanities of Bayreuth. His attraction lay in Balakirev, Borodin and Rimsky-Korsakov. His romantic feelings were stirred by the imaginative colour of *A Thousand and One Nights* and he decided to compose an opera—*Shéhérazade*.

The plot was gruesome enough in all conscience. Shahrazad begins to tell one of her stories (Sindbad the Sailor) surrounded by the corpses of previous sultanas. The sultan begins to nod. The executioners approach with the fatal cord. . . . Ravel soon got tired of this and turned to a story by Hoffmann called *Olympia*, upon which Offenbach based one of the acts of his famous *Tales* and Delibes the ballet *Coppélia*. Ravel was drawn to it by reason of his growing love for mechanical toys, the seeds of which had been planted at the Exposition Universelle.

The overture to *Shéhérazade* was performed for the first time on 27th May 1899 by the orchestra of the Société Nationale. Ravel conducted it himself. The audience whistled. The critics were furious. Never had such noises emanated before from a respectable orchestra—and the Société Nationale was a very respectable association. It was founded in 1871 by Romain Bussine, a professor of singing at the Conservatoire, and Camille Saint-Saëns. It started with the laudable policy of affording French composers an opportunity of hearing their own works and fighting the prevailing obsession with operatic music. Its whole purpose was to try to formulate a national style and thus draw French music away from the influence of Wagner. This was all to the good, and much excellent music was played for the first time, including one of César Franck's trios, which also was received with disapprobation! Its influence was tremendous. In this country we might draw an analogy with the Patron's Fund, with the difference that the latter was concerned more with unknown and untried music than with the formulation of any style. The Société Nationale found the overture to *Shéhérazade* a little too much for it. Pierre Lalo saw in the work the influence of Grieg (!), Rimsky-Korsakov and/or Balakirev and complained that the characteristics of these composers were carried to excess, to the point of vice, by Ravel. He also said that if Ravel considered this an overture, 'constructed after a classical plan,' he must be credited with a vivid imagination.

Ravel was discouraged by this reception but, like all enthusiasts, easily threw off his depression. A few years later he used some of the material in a setting of poems by his friend Tristan Klingsor, under the same title.

The year 1899 saw the composition of the first of those works which have made the name of Ravel a household matter. It may be that the *Pavane pour une Infante défunte* (even now still referred to sometimes as being 'for a dead *child*') is not great music and is not truly representative of the Ravel we know. It may be that M. Roland-Manuel is right when he speaks slightingly of it as suitable for 'young girls.' [1] What is significant about it is that we see traces of his Basque origin once more. The whole *raison d'être* of the work is the stately pavan danced in front of the bier of a Spanish princess, which dance was a characteristic one of old Spain. The music itself, although not startlingly original as we hear things now, is personal enough to be recognizable as Ravel's, for reasons which we shall see presently.

[1] *A la Gloire de Ravel*, 1938.

In 1901 Ravel decided to try for the Prix de Rome. The text of the cantata *Myrrha* was by Fernand Boussier. Ravel approached the matter with becoming gravity (?), regarding it in the light of a game. What the examiners thought and said when they came across a *Valse lente* must be left to the imagination; but Ravel was too obviously full of promise to be ignored. He was awarded the second prize, the first going to André Caplet.

We may pause here awhile to consider the Prix de Rome and its winners. It is the blue ribbon of music in France, but the depressing thing is that few of the winners have ever done anything to justify themselves. Granted that our knowledge of French music is not nearly as complete as we like to think it is, the list of names makes melancholy reading. The same thing must apply to everything of this nature, but with the Prix de Rome the list of those who have never done anything since receiving the award is utterly out of proportion to the names who have made the grade. Looking down the list of those whose names will appear in these pages, we find the following: Pessard, Caplet, Leroux, Vidal, Lenepveu, Hillemacher (two of them), Debussy. Of these, how many may be said to have justified themselves? Caplet is a composer of whom we are aware but of whose music we know nothing. He conducted *Pelléas et Mélisande* at Covent Garden in 1912. Although we boast of our 'Great English Choral Tradition,' I doubt if *Le Miroir de Jésus* is in the repertories of our cathedrals or if the organists of our cathedrals and large parish churches have ever heard of it. Caplet was wounded and gassed in the last war, dying in 1925. Debussy's is the only other name of any note.

André Cœuroy, giving the list of winners up to 1923 in Dent's *Dictionary of Modern Music and Musicians*, ends up his paragraph by saying that 'since 1880 many really good French musicians have not had the Prix.'

There is often irony in this kind of thing, academicism not always seeing eye to eye with creation. Many years ago a now famous British composer scored an enormous success with an orchestral work on the evening of the day he failed to pass an examination in the elements of music! Evidently the task of writing the correct number of semi-demi-semiquavers in an *adagio* trill proved too exacting!

The humour of the situation lies in the fact that Ravel had composed and published *Jeux d'eau*. The effect of this work was startling, and Ravel seemed quite horrified at what he had done. After the poor reception accorded his earlier works, it seemed incredible that at last something was received with almost universal approval; even the jaundiced Pierre Lalo praised it. Debussy studied it with minute attention, and his subsequent treatment of the piano proved that he had learned a lot from it, both musically and from the point of view of technique. Up to that time Debussy's only significant piano work was the suite *Pour le Piano*, and even then the *Sarabande*, later orchestrated by Ravel, was the only movement of importance. Ravel showed at once that France had a composer with a natural bent for the piano.

Ravel had by this time become established among the young artists of the day, and his friends included many exponents of the most advanced thought. The French have always had a *penchant* for cliques and associations, not necessarily confined to one particular art. Ravel, at an impressionable age, found himself on terms of familiarity with names such as Tristan Klingsor, Charles Guérin, Florent Schmitt, Ingelbrecht, Séverac, André Caplet, Manuel de Falla and Igor Stravinsky. This association discussed music, painting and literature with all the sincerity of enthusiasm. They went as a body to hear all the enterprising music they could find, including *Pelléas et Mélisande*. It was at this performance that they adopted a name for themselves. Entering the theatre, they heard a newsagent crying out: 'Attention! Les apaches!' Ricardo Viñes replied: 'Nous, nous sommes les apaches!' and the name stuck. In due course they adopted also a kind of signature tune, the subject of Borodin's second Symphony, and the whistling of this was a rallying signal. It also had the advantage of letting each member who heard it outside his window know that work would be over for that day or night. They met at various houses and to the neighbours made night quite horrible.

During the years 1902-3 Ravel was occupied with his first extended work, the string Quartet in F major. This work, so gracious and charming that it might have been written by Fauré, yet bears the unmistakable stamp of Ravel all over. It made as big an impression as the similar work by Debussy. Ravel had doubts about the last movement, but Debussy ordered him not to change a single note.

Undaunted by his previous failure, he determined to sit once more for the Prix de Rome, with the cantata *Alcyone*. He failed. In 1903 he tried again, with *Alyssa*. He failed again.

In between times he turned his attention to a set of poems by his brother Apache Tristan Klingsor, entitled *Shéhérazade*. They were performed for the first time by Jane Hatto at a concert of the Société Nationale.

Although he was not really anxious for the Prix de Rome, he felt that, having tried three times, a fourth would do no harm; also, he felt that he was under some kind of academic obligation to Fauré. He submitted his name in 1905. Then the balloon went up. He had not reckoned with the backwash of his rebellious student days. 'M. Ravel may consider us *pompiers*[1]: he shall not take us for imbeciles with impunity.' Thus spoke a member of the committee. Ravel was not allowed to enter.

Fortunately the names of the jury were not in any way 'top security,' and we are able to judge the situation from their names and the positions they hold in musical history. They were Charles Lenepveu, Théodore Dubois, Émile Paladilhe, Jules Massenet and Ernest Reyer, representing the Institut, with Xavier Leroux, Hillemacher and Roujon as co-opted members. Of

[1] Meaning literally 'firemen' or 'pump-workers.' It is used in a contemptuous sense and we have no English equivalent printable without giving offence. *Faire son pompier*, in studio slang, means to paint a large picture with someone in it in full classical armour, suggestive of a fireman.

13

these, only one is of any note (Massenet) while another (Dubois) was, as will be remembered, one of Ravel's earliest teachers. Jean Marnold of the *Mercure de France* took up cudgels on behalf of the composer of the Quartet in F, 'one of the masters of to morrow.' He also brought to light the startling fact that all the candidates whose entries had been accepted were pupils of Lenepveu, and he asked if in future the Prix de Rome was to be 'extorted by intrigue or awarded by idiots.'

The press in general took up the matter, and other individuals, particularly Romain Rolland. 'L'affaire Ravel' rose to a climax. The ultimate result was that Théodore Dubois resigned his posi tion as head of the Conservatoire and Gabriel Fauré reigned in his stead. There was only one person unmoved. While the battle was at its height, Ravel was yachting in Holland.

The trip to Holland did not start without some incident. Ravel had been asked to write something for the harp. Being thorough in his methods, he probed the mysteries of the instru ment to their depths and set to work on what was to be the *Introduction and Allegro* for harp with accompaniment for string quartet, flute and clarinet. He decided to take the manuscript with him, and before embarking on the yacht at Soissons went to an outfitter to buy 'suitable shirts for nautical wear.' In the shop he was so overcome by a hat of unique shape and proportions that he left the manuscript on the counter, and his friends recovered it from the owner of the shop, who was a great lover of music.

Maurice Delage in telling this story [1] quotes a letter he received, testifying to the joy which Ravel was taking in the voyage, written in the port of Amsterdam:

We have been here for three days, and I have not yet visited the museums. There are so many things to see! To day a most magni ficent sight: a lake fringed with windmills. In the fields, windmills, as far as the eye could see. In every direction we looked, we saw nothing but turning wheels. One finished up by thinking one had become an automaton oneself, such a 'mechanical' journey had it become.

---

[1] *Maurice Ravel*, by Some of his Friends.

After all that, I need not say that I have accomplished nothing. But I am gestating, and I believe that a heap of things will result from this tour.

He was right. Many things did result from it during the next three years: the piano Sonatina and *Miroirs* (1905), *Introduction and Allegro*, *Histoires naturelles* (1906), *Rapsodie espagnole* and *L'Heure espagnole* (1907).

Each of these works marks a significance in Ravel's progress and two, at least, are familiar names in this country. The Sonatina was composed for a competition organized by a musical journal and, consequently, was published immediately and knowledge of it spread far and wide without any difficulty. Its slight texture made an instant appeal; over here it introduced him to a very wide circle.

His thoughts were constantly occupied with the piano. Debussy remarked to Ricardo Viñes at a meeting of the 'Apaches' that he wanted to write music which should be so free that it would appear to have been improvised. Ravel overheard this. At the time he was known as 'the composer of *Jeux d'eau*,' and this was distressing him, since he had no mind to become a one-work composer. A little later he showed Viñes the set of five piano pieces known collectively as *Miroirs*. The first to be played was *Oiseaux tristes*, and on hearing this André Suarès said [1] that 'if it were possible for music to paint an object without first disclosing it, Ravel's succeeded better than any other.' This certainly applies to more works than *Miroirs*, but it is a remarkable penetration into Ravel's mind.

Browsing on the Quai bookstalls, Ravel picked up a copy of Gerhart Hauptmann's play *Die versunkene Glocke*, translated as *La Cloche engloutie* by A. F. Hérold. The word *cloche* seemed always to go to his head, and he decided to make a musical setting of the work. He took the book to Lavallois and on 12th June 1906 he wrote to Maurice Delage, telling him [2] that he had never worked with such frenzy.

[1] Roland-Manuel, *A la Gloire de Ravel*.
[2] *Maurice Ravel*, by Some of his Friends.

About this time his father fell ill and it was necessary for him to go to Switzerland. Maurice was deeply attached to his parents, so, packing up *La Cloche engloutie*, he accompanied the invalid to Hermance on Lake Geneva. The fever of work died down and some more pressing ideas made him put the manuscript away. He worked at it in a desultory manner for some years, but in 1914 abandoned it altogether. Some of the material he used in Act II of *L'Enfant et les sortilèges*. This habit of abandoning works is common to all composers. Ravel seems to have been one of those least afflicted with it.

Now came the second *affaire*. He had long been working at the poems of Jules Renard and eventually finished five of them under the collective title of *Histoires naturelles*. They were per-formed at a concert of the Société Nationale. Let us give that society full credit. It may not have liked the 'new thought,' but at least it performed it and gave French composers the oppor-tunities which all composers deserve and have the right to expect. The singer was Jane Bathori. The songs were received with cat-calls, whistles and jeers, but in spite of everything the singer stuck to the songs with commendable pertinacity. This *affaire* is considered to have emanated from a certain source, and to understand the situation we must look at musical Paris of that time.

To get a reasonable perspective, imagine the Royal College and the Royal Academy of Music in terms of complete antithesis and the position becomes clear.

The faction which ruled music in Paris with the Conservatoire, although opposed fundamentally to the principles of that institu-tion, was the Schola Cantorum founded by Charles Bordes, Alexandre Guilmant and Vincent d'Indy. This institution based its teaching and gospel on those of César Franck. Every-thing about Ravel was hostile to the Schola Cantorum, his own outlook, his teachers, Gédalge and Fauré and his idol, Debussy. He himself was utterly out of sympathy with the gods of the Schola—Franck, Wagner and Beethoven. He had no use for

Wagner and admired Beethoven with reservations. His 'heroes' were certainly a queer bunch—Mozart, Gounod(!) and, in the matter of technique, Saint-Saëns. The two, therefore, were poles apart.

Here is Charles Koechlin's version of what happened: [1]

In the venerable society founded by Saint-Saens and Romain Bussine, it was the spirit of the Schola which prevailed. It unleashed itself vehemently, that evening, in a stormy revolt against Ravellian conciseness. To start with, one part of the audience was hostile. It behaved itself in execrable taste at this humour, which it judged 'devoid of music'; the silent bars of *Grillon*, above all, called forth jeers. And when, at the opening bars of the mysterious and marvellous *Martin-pêcheur* Jane Bathori sang the phrase 'Ça n'a pas mordu, ce soir,' with what low and coarse laughter was it received! The Ravellians, and even the more 'neutral' listeners were exasperated by this unqualified attitude. They promised themselves that they would not forget it. I was amongst them. I have not forgotten it yet. Nor you, either, Jane Bathori——

The press, of course, was terrific. The critics could not see that the songs were humorous! Auguste Sérieyx and his friends from the Schola were determined to fight 'without mercy.' Pierre Lalo heard in the songs an echo of Debussy. Immediately Jean Marnold, Louis Laloy, G. Jean-Aubry and M. D. Calvocoressi rose to the occasion. The last-named pointed out that it was as silly to accuse Ravel of copying Debussy as to accuse Weber, Beethoven and Schubert of copying each other. This second *affaire Ravel* pursued its way. Ravel himself went to Valvins, where he composed the *Rapsodie espagnole* in thirty days. Roland-Manuel describes *Histoires naturelles* as an exercise in declamation. The *Rapsodie espagnole* he calls a study for orchestra. [2]

It will be remembered that in 1895 Ravel wrote an *Habanera* for two pianos which was never published. This piece he

---

[1] *La Revue musicale,* December 1938.
[2] *A la Gloire de Ravel.*

included in the *Rapsodie espagnole* as the third movement—without altering a single note. The first performance was conducted by Ravel himself on 28th March 1908 at one of the Concerts Colonne. Colonne felt that he was too old to manage this intricate box of musical tricks. The audience was divided. Those 'upstairs' vociferously encored the second movement, *Malagueña,* while those 'downstairs' equally vociferously whistled. Above the tumult the voice of Florent Schmitt was heard shouting that the move, ment should be played once again for the benefit of those down, stairs who did not understand it.

Truly, things were alive in those days.

Between May and September 1907 Ravel was delighting him, self with the composition of an opera, *L'Heure espagnole*, in which he let his mechanical fancies run riot. The libretto was just the kind to stimulate his genius: it was witty, naughty—and mechani, cal! Ravel's enthusiasm received rather a damper when he played the work through to the librettist, Franc, Nohain. On turning round for some opinion there was silence for a moment. Then Franc, Nohain pulled out his watch, looked at it and said: 'Fifty, six minutes.' He was not interested in music.

Production was delayed for some years. Albert Carré, the director of the Opéra, Comique, had scruples and fears that it might be labelled 'obscene.' Eventually it was performed in 1911.

CHAPTER III

MATURITY (1908-14)

AT this time Ravel was indulging his taste for *bibelots* and mechanical toys. The tiny mechanism of these toys fascinated him
and formed the counterpart of his diminutive self and dapper
appearance. A photograph of the period shows him with a trim
beard, a flowery shirt and smartly cut suit. He might almost
have been a mechanical toy himself.

He was attracted by the illustrations to an edition of fairy-
tales by Perrault, Mme d'Aulnoy and Mme Leprince de Beaumont. Ravel's friends Ida and Cipa Godebski, in whose house
the 'Apaches' held their meetings, had two children, Mimi
and Jean. He found an inspiration in these children which had
its outlet in the suite for piano duet *Ma Mère l'Oye*, the music of
which was closely allied to the spirit of the illustrations. It was
necessary to simplify his natural style for these pieces, but there is
no sign of effort or self-conscious descent to the required level of
simplicity. The pieces are unique not only in the list of Ravel's
achievements, but in music generally, where we search in vain
for anything of the kind so wholly satisfactory; the balance
between the slenderness of the tales and the slightness of the
musical technique is perfect and the musical characterization
infallible. Later the suite was used as a ballet.

From this simplicity, if not naïvety, Ravel turned to something
very different. If Perrault suggested a tiny suite for piano duet,
Louis Bertrand suggested a set of three pieces in which Ravel
extended his piano technique to its limit. 'White magic to
black.' [1] From childhood's easy background to one of power,
depth and tragedy. He expressed to Maurice Delage the
desire to write some pieces on the same level of virtuosity as

[1] Roland-Manuel, *A la Gloire de Ravel*.

19

Balakirev's *Islamey*. The requirements for that work are of a brilliant order. Those required for *Gaspard de la Nuit* are a sure technique and wide musical imagination. Ravel carried the range of the piano to its utmost limit and used the instrument in a manner usually associated with the orchestra. The three movements are worthy to rank with the finest music. *Ondine* is treated in a way different from Debussy's; *Le Gibet*, with its swaying syncopated pedal-point, graphically describes the figure of the robber hanging in chains; in *Scarbo* we can see the little scratching figure in all its antics. Ravel had reached the highest pinnacle in contemporary music.

The same year saw the death of Joseph Ravel, his father, to whom he was devoted.

In 1909 he wrote a *pièce d'occasion* of no great moment, the *Menuet sur le nom d'Haydn* for piano, but the year was remarkable for the phenomenon of the Russian Ballet which Sergey Diaghilev was taking round Europe. This was something completely new. For the first time the culture of the land of mystery was brought out into the light, and it was a revelation. The names of Bakst, Benois, Roerich and Fokin were first heard of by the general theatre-going public, and the blaze of colour which the rising of the curtain displayed took every one's breath away.

Here were seen for the first time the true union of painting and movement, backed up by the element of music—*Les Sylphides, Prince Igor*, names so familiar now but then only just beginning to be known, and an impresario who had taste and ambitions. Diaghilev inquired who were the leading French composers and was directed to Ravel. Fokin showed Ravel the scenario of *Daphnis et Chloé*. Ravel was delighted at the prospect of writing a work for the Russian Ballet, but was not altogether satisfied with the script. He found it 'feeble.' His corrections and alterations were approved by Fokin, and the music was begun.

Ravel went to Valvins and settled down in a villa belonging to his friends the Godebskis. Here he worked hard, regardless

'La Revue Musicale'

QUAI DE LA NIVELLE, CIBOURE, LATER NAMED QUAI MAURICE RAVEL

of outside distractions. The floods rose, but he did not notice them. He was found writing with the water all round him; but the work did not progress very fast, and it was not till 1912 that it was completed.

As often happens when a composer is engaged on an extended work, that work is interrupted by other thoughts and oppor-tunities. *Daphnis et Chloé* was interrupted in 1910 by the com-position of some Greek popular songs, and in 1911 by the now famous *Valses nobles et sentimentales*.

Musicians generally were disgusted with the Société Nationale, and some of the rebels, headed by Gabriel Fauré, decided to inaugurate an opposition scheme. This was known as the Société Musicale Indépendante, and its first concert was given on 20th April 1910, at which *Ma Mère l'Oye* received its first per-formance. On 16th January 1911 Ravel took part in a concert devoted to the works of Erik Satie. The same year saw a notable venture on the part of the new society. It was decided to give a concert of music by anonymous composers and to note the reactions of the audience. In this way there would be no bias whatsoever against names to which some might take exception. The leading composers of the day entered into the spirit of the game, and only the performers knew whose music was being played. Louis Aubert, himself a composer of no mean notability, played Ravel's work, *Valses nobles et sentimentales*.

Then the fun began. There was the usual whistling, but Ravel kept admirable patience during the performance and the ensuing discussion. The audience had been provided with pieces of paper on which they were to write the names of those who they thought were the composers of all the music. A surprising list of guesses resulted. The works other than Ravel's were ascribed to Mozart, Schumann, Chopin, Gounod and Mendelssohn,[1] while the *Valses* were ascribed to Kodály, Satie and Théodore Dubois.[2] It is difficult to see how any sane listener could ascribe

[1] Émile Vuillermoz, *Maurice Ravel*, by Some of his Friends.
[2] Roland-Manuel, *A la Gloire de Ravel*.

these progressive works to any of 'the great masters.' The pro-
fessional critics refrained from guessing [1]—how prudent they were!

It is indeed difficult to-day to see how the *Valses nobles et
sentimentales* could have upset anybody. Ravel himself said: [1]

> The title, *Valses nobles et sentimentales*, shows clearly enough my
> intention to compose a chain of valses in the style of Schubert. In
> place of the virtuosity which characterized *Gaspard de le Nuit*, there was
> a style cleaner, clearer, which emphasized the harmonies and brought
> them into relief.

Ravel was drawn to Vienna: the work first named *Wien* (and
later *La Valse*) was intended as a picture of the city as he himself saw it.

Meanwhile *L'Heure espagnole* had been finished and published
in 1910. Under pressure from an influential patron, Mme Jean
Cruppi, it was produced by Albert Carré at the Opéra-Comique
on 19th May 1911. Being a short work it shared the bill with
Massenet's *Thérèse*—of all things. Needless to say, there was another storm from the critics, although the audience was at least
polite. The inevitable Pierre Lalo, no friend to Ravellian enter-
prises, saw a similarity with Debussy in those places where the
music was picturesque and illustrative. He disliked the declamatory use of the voice and found that the only good point of the
work was the use of the orchestra. An extract from his article
in *Le Temps*, dated 28th May 1911, will give us the gist:

> Everything is ice and ice-bound; and everything is small, minute,
> tight, scanty: the stature, movement, gestures, text even, and its accent.
> This inanimate, artificial, mechanical and ice-bound atmosphere . . .

Plainly Pierre Lalo did not admire *L'Heure espagnole*. The
opposition to him was heard in the voices of Émile Vuillermoz
and Henri Ghéon. These critics were not concerned with tracing
pedigrees or finding parallels with other composers. They were
content to see a score definitely breaking away from Wagner and
preaching a gospel truly and veritably French.

The next year (1912) saw Ravel completely occupied with

[1] Biographical Sketch.

ballets. Jacques Rouché decided to produce *L'Heure espagnole* at the Opéra, but in the meanwhile commissioned Ravel to make a ballet from the Suite *Ma Mère l'Oye*. Ravel himself devised the scenario, bringing all the movements into the story of *The Sleeping Beauty*. He added a prelude and four interludes. It was all too small for the Opéra stage, but M. Rouché had other plans. It was performed at the Arts Theatre and took the form of a divertissement, making a delicious contrast to the ballets of Musset, Roussel and other composers.

The *Valses nobles et sentimentales* were orchestrated in a fortnight and performed on 22nd April 1912 at the Châtelet. The performance was given by Natalia Trukhanova and the programme seems long enough to satisfy the most rapacious ballet fan—*Istar* (Vincent d'Indy), *The Tragedy of Salome* (Florent Schmitt) and *La Péri* (Paul Dukas). Ravel's work went under the title of *Adelaide, or the Language of Flowers*. Each composer conducted his own work. Ravel was not a great conductor, but comforted himself that as the music was always in triple time, it would be all right once he had started. He had forgotten the intricate rhythms of the seventh valse!

During 1911 the score of *Daphnis et Chloé* was partly finished. It received a 'try-out' at a private concert, and after the Bacchanal had been recast the work was terminated on 5th April 1912.

The publisher, Jacques Durand, told Diaghilev that everything was ready for rehearsals and production; but Diaghilev hesitated. He was not satisfied with the work as a whole. To start with, it was not written in ballet form and had not been composed 'round the table' with the choreographer. The basis was melodic rather than rhythmic. Further, the high-light of the season was *L'Après-midi*, another Greek ballet round which scandal and indignation had run riot. *L'Après-midi* was static; *Daphnis et Chloé* intensely mobile. Durand brought all his powers of persuasion into play, and eventually Diaghilev relented. A period of storm ensued.

M. Durand gives us a personal insight into the situation:[1]

As what was being said was in Russian, I could only hear the tone of voice, which was violent. Some questions about the choreography arose; they appeared to be diametrically opposed to each other. I know only what was finally settled.

The music was extremely difficult for the dancers. Sergey Lifar says [2] that the only way they could grasp the 5–8 rhythm of the finale was to repeat the syllables 'Ser-gey-Dia-ghi-lev.' Other complications arose. Fokin could not dismiss from his mind the *Prince Igor* dances, and the 'Danse guerrière' in *Daphnis* was too reminiscent of the older work. Further, the re-enacting of the scene between Pan and Syrinx was treated in mime instead of as a *pas de deux*. It would appear that the score was beyond the choreographer's resources.

Cyril Beaumont gives us the information [3] that the libretto was a portion of a two-act ballet which Fokin wished to produce in 1904 and for which Bakst had designed the scenery. *Daphnis* consisted of the first act, divided into three scenes, from this libretto. The costumes for *Daphnis* were picked out from other ballets, including *Narcisse*. In spite of the commissioned score, it would appear that the production fell short with its *décor*, for dished-up scenery and costumes are never the same as those designed especially for a particular work.

The first performance took place on 8th June 1912. The performers were not ready. Mr. Beaumont tells us that on 5th June the finale had not been arranged. Fokin hurriedly decided on certain movements which were suitable for the rush, if not for posterity; they have not been altered.

It was not an unqualified success. The season had been sensational for the scandal of *L'Après-midi*. The uproar had died down, but the memory of the ballet remained. Nizhinsky had

[1] *Memories of a Music Publisher*, vol. i.
[2] *La Revue musicale*, December 1938.
[3] *Michael Fokin and his Ballets*.

broken fresh ground with the Debussy work, and the public was
fixed in its ideas of what a Greek setting should be.

In spite of the musical splendour of the ballet, in spite of the dancing
of the *corps*, extremely beautiful and certainly inspired by Fokin, sometimes real 'creations,' it was not an event. Perhaps the ballet was
eclipsed by the *clou* of the season, *L'Après-midi d'un faune*; perhaps also
the absence of harmony between the music, the *décor* and the choreography, perhaps the interpretation was too literal. . . .

So suggests Sergey Lifar.[1] In any case, a coldness arose
between Diaghilev and Ravel, and it was not till 1917 that
tentative suggestions were made for another collaboration.

Whatever the hits and kicks which were distributed so lavishly
behind the scenes, the public and the critics were concerned with
the music, and where this aspect of the work was considered the
reaction was distinctly favourable. Robert Brussel in the *Figaro*
wrote that *Daphnis et Chloé* was the most finished, the most
poetic work which Diaghilev's enterprise had produced:

One was usually dazzled by M. Ravel; one is now almost thrilled
by an infinitely sweet, fresh tenderness, as beseems such a subject.

Émile Vuillermoz wrote equally enthusiastically; but Gaston
Carraud found certain elements lacking, particularly rhythm,
which he described as 'weak' and not giving the impression of
movement in its truest sense.

The work was not performed again until 1913, and when the
'Ballets Russes' disbanded it disappeared with them. Finally it
was acquired *in toto* by the Paris Opéra, where it is still played.

We may reflect upon various points in this history. Perhaps
that which strikes us most is the impossibility of producing a 'work
of art' in the theatre without constant alarums and excursions.
From our point of view (which, of course, is concerned mainly
with the music) it is almost tragic that a great score, containing
such beauties, such strength, such individuality, should be hedged

[1] *La Revue musicale,* December 1938.

round with the petty bickerings and jealousies of personalities. Art is always supposed to be uplifting . . .

In 1913 Ravel was fully established as the leader of French musical expression. His missionaries, Jane Bathori and Ricardo Viñes, preached his gospel wherever they went, and with maturity in music there sprang up a different personality. Roland-Manuel remarks on Ravel's decision to dispense with a beard. To some the addition of a beard gives distinction. To Ravel the removal of it gave him added dignity.

Although not inclined to commission another ballet, Diaghilev gave Ravel the unfinished opera of *Khovanshtchina* by Mussorgsky to orchestrate, in conjunction with Stravinsky. Stravinsky was then living at Clarens, whither Ravel went to join him. They lived in separate hotels, but met frequently to discuss their work. A great friendship sprung up between them which, later, Stravinsky was to repudiate maliciously by referring to Ravel as an *horloge suisse*. Ravel found Stravinsky's *Poèmes de la lyrique iaponaise* and was much intrigued by them. Stravinsky explained that they had been suggested by Schoenberg's *Pierrot lunaire*. Ravel conceived the idea of setting three of Mallarmé's poems for voice, piano, string quartet, two flutes and two clarinets. Here his intention was not so much to write songs with accompaniment for chamber *ensemble* as to include the voice with the chamber-music combination.

While at Clarens Ravel played *The Rite of Spring,* then unpublished, on the piano with Stravinsky. The work roused all his enthusiasm and he wrote to Lucien Garban that he considered the performance of this work would be as important an event as that of *Pelléas*. On 29th May 1913 he took part in the 'battle of *Le Sacre*,' at which Florent Schmitt performed as vocal a part as he played after the first performance of the *Rapsodie espagnole*.

The year 1913 saw also the composition of a small Prelude for piano and two unneccessary parodies of Borodin and Chabrier, amusing in their way, but entirely pointless.[1]

[1] Published, with others by Alfredo Casella, as *A la manière de . . .*

It is always interesting to find performers reacting to composers who are in their heyday but seemingly still unknown in certain quarters; one would expect that Ravel was a familiar name and figure in all musical circles. Let us hear Madeleine Grey on this point: [1]

At my first orchestral concert, having sung under the conductorship of Rhené-Baton at a Concert Pasdeloup, I saw in the vestibule an elegant little man approach me—clad in black-and-white check, with a straw hat and stick. He congratulated me in the usual manner, at the same time very discreetly and warmly, and asked me if I should like to work at certain songs which would suit me particularly. On inquiring the name of this *petit monsieur*, I was not aware of the honour which he did me, for I only vaguely knew his music.

In no way annoyed that a singer who made her début at symphony concerts should not be better acquainted with the 'young' music, Ravel made a promise, and I received from him the famous *Chansons hébraïques* which aroused my enthusiasm and which I went to sing at Saint-Cloud. I returned with some white roses which he had cut for me.

It seems quite peculiar that any singer should not have heard of Ravel's songs, have not even heard of the *affaire* of the *Histoires naturelles*, and still more, not have heard of *Daphnis et Chloé* or any of the other works which had caused such storms of indignation. Do singers live in ivory towers? It was these *Chansons hébraïques* which gave Ravel's detractors the opportunity of accusing him of Semitic origin!

Ravel was always impressed with the clarity and technique of Camille Saint-Saëns, although not in any way influenced by that composer in the matter of style or idiom. He sketched out a piano concerto on Basque themes—*Zispiak Bat*—but found that although he had used 'national' airs in some songs, he could not get at the right Basque spirit. He gave up the idea of the Concerto, but used the theme in his Trio for violin, cello and piano, one of the monumental works of its kind.

In 1914 the first world war broke out.

[1] *La Revue musicale*, December 1938.

CHAPTER IV

THE WAR AND AFTER (1914–22)

RAVEL was liable for military service, like any one else, but his calling-up papers did not arrive and he grew impatient. Although he knew that he served France by composing music, he was not prepared to hide behind that refuge for any definite or indefinite space of time. His friend Tristan Klingsor, brother-Apache and poet of *Schéhérezade,* had been mobilized from the very first, and Raval besought him to use his influence with the head of military affairs in the department of the Seine.

Klingsor hesitated. He had lost several of his friends and felt that if the state would not call Ravel up, it was not for him to do anything about it. Ravel became so pressing that in the end he arranged for him to be medically examined. He was turned down. This in no way daunted him. Into the army he wished to go and nothing would alter his decision. Other musicians were in the forces and he felt out of things. In spite of bad health Roussel had gone as an ambulance driver, later becoming an artillery officer, and there was the tragedy of 'poor Magnard' to avenge. This tragedy is worth recalling.

Albéric Magnard was a composer of solid style who was completely oblivious of the world around him. He cared for neither fame nor performance and concentrated entirely on his work. At the beginning of September 1914 he saw two Uhlans in his garden at Baron (Oise). He promptly shot them, and was shot in return, his house being burnt to the ground with all his manuscripts.

Ravel persisted and eventually managed to convince M. Paul Painlevé that although his light weight might make him unsuitable for the infantry, it was just the thing for the air force. He was accepted in 1915.

In the meantime he had been forced to serve France only as a

IN THE FRENCH ARMY

composer by completing the Trio. He had abandoned *La Cloche engloutie*, begun with such frenzy in 1905, and also *Zispiak Bat*, the proposed piano Concerto. He had started *Wien*, and was full of other ideas—a *Suite française* afterwards known as *Le Tombeau de Couperin*, and a *Romantic Night*, full of 'dismals,' demon-hunters, accursed nuns, etc.[1] This last venture came to nothing. The work on the Trio kept him fully occupied, however, and when in the end he left for his military service, there was nothing outstanding except the sketches for *Wien*. From this moment until his discharge in 1917 he ceased practically to have anything to do with music, although managing to work sporadically at *Trois Chansons* for mixed chorus.

He had no military ambitions. As he wrote to Roland-Manuel (who was at the Dardanelles) in 1915, he had so far run no risk of getting the Croix de Guerre. His heart and lungs were good, and after a year of camp life he passed into the air force. He left for the front, at Verdun, on 14th March 1916, in charge of a convoy; thus the composer of the exquisite *Ma Mère l'Oye* and the Quartet found himself face to face with stern reality.

Fortunately he had a sense of humour which stiffened his sensitiveness. He was asked to sing some of his music at a camp concert, but considered that the *Trois Poèmes de Mallarmé* would hardly be satisfactory in the circumstances, and begged to be excused. In the midst of the fighting he found time to take up cudgels against a movement which had sprung up in Paris and had its echoes in other countries. There arose a society called the Ligue Nationale pour la Défense de la Musique Française which determined to forbid the performance of all music of enemy origin for the duration of the war. Ravel's friend, Jean Marnold, strenuously opposed this in the *Mercure de France*. The league also tried to deny the right of all creative artists not mobilized to pursue their calling during the period of hostilities. M. Marnold replied that Sophocles produced a trilogy during the Peloponnesian

[1] Roland-Manuel, *A la Gloire de Ravel*.

War. A woman writer counter-attacked with the astonishing statement that it would appear that 'nobody heard the cannon.' Ravel, who was hearing the cannon all day and every day, was drawn into the argument and wrote a lengthy letter to the secretary of the association, in which he said: [1]

It matters little that M. Schoenberg, for example, should be of Austrian nationality. He is no less a musician of high merit whose experiments, full of interest, have had a happy influence on certain allied composers and on ours. Further, I am entranced that MM. Bartók, Kodály and their disciples should be Hungarians, and should show it in their works with such relish.

In Germany, apart from M. Richard Strauss, we find only composers of the second rank, whose equivalent it would be easy to find without crossing frontiers. But it is possible that soon some young artists will arise whom it will be interesting to know here.

Ravel informed the president that he did not wish his name to appear among his members. The president took a poor view of this and breathed forth threatenings and slaughter, quoting as among the supporters of the Ligue the names of Saint-Saëns, Charpentier and d'Indy; it is hard to give credence to the inclusion of the last-named, an ardent admirer of the German classics. The first was, of course, in his dotage and the second did not matter.

The Ligue, however, did not stop there. It ran a campaign against Wagner which was strenuously combated by M. Marnold. In his book *Le Cas Wagner*, published in 1920, he quotes a number of letters received from the troops in support of his pro-Wagner activities, particularly one from an artillery officer stating categorically that 'We will not allow the composer of *Tristan* to be banned in our country.'

This, of course, happened in the recent war also, but there politics entered in very strongly. There was no lack of Beethoven and others; only Wagner was discreetly allowed to rest, he being considered a true Nazi. Indeed, at the beginning of the war a

[1] *La Revue musicale*, December 1938.

member of the French embassy in London was heard to remark that since the war began England had become the stronghold of German music. The iniquity lay in the possibility of living German composers eventually receiving performing and hiring fees and thus depriving British and allied composers of their rightful dues. However, the supply of Nazi music was never notable for either its quality or quantity, and the Fascist Italian composers were never missed. The number of British composers in the forces naturally found their activities curtailed, but those whose 'consciences' made them serve England by composing instead of taking an active part, in no matter how small a way, reaped a rich harvest. One can only hope that they enjoyed themselves.

Ravel's military career was undistinguished, as such careers are understood, but he seems to have had an affray with a policeman for which he was given a short period of detention behind the line. In May 1916 he went through another medical inspection, and it was found that his health was in a bad state. He was depressed at the news he received about his mother, for whom he had a lively affection. Absence from music also made him miserable. 'I believed I had forgotten it,' he wrote;[1] but later, 'I have never been so musical. I overflow with inspiration, for plans of all kinds, chamber music, symphonies.'[1] He found only one solution, 'the end of the war,' but he in no way failed in his duties. 'Decidedly an artist is intended to fight, but surely not to lead barrack life.'[1] At Châlons-sur-Marne on 6th September he fell ill and was taken to hospital.

He went to Paris to convalesce, and on 5th January 1917 his mother died. Ravel was heart-broken and for a time lived in a state of stupor. A month later he rejoined his unit at Châlons, where he was bored to death. He needed action and movement. The ordinary training and routine life got him down as it gets every one, but in June the musical instincts in him came to life again and he asked his friend Lucien Garban to send

[1] Letters quoted in *A la Gloire de Ravel*, Roland-Manuel.

him Liszt's *Études d'exécution transcendante*, *Mazeppa* and *Feux follets*.

It will be remembered that before he was called up he planned a *Suite française* for piano. In 1917 he finished the suite *Le Tombeau de Couperin*, of which he said that it was 'Homage less, in reality, to Couperin himself than to eighteenth-century French music.' [1] Each movement is dedicated to a friend killed in the war. He appeared to take a last farewell to the style of his youth, and Roland-Manuel sees in the *Rigaudon* a kinship with the early *Menuet antique* and Sonatina.[2] Two years later he orchestrated four numbers of the suite—another instance of the pliability of his pianistic technique.

In 1916 Colette wrote a libretto for a divertimento called *Ballet for my Daughter*, which she showed to M. Rouché of the Opéra. The latter suggested Ravel as the composer. She posted a copy to the composer while he was in the army, but it never reached him. As soon as Ravel was released M. Rouché sent for him and proposed Colette's libretto as a suitable work. Roland-Manuel says [3] that Ravel at first declined the invitation because he had not got a daughter and the title seemed to him inappro-priate. However, with a certain amount of pressure he eventually consented, and the work was renamed *L'Enfant et les sortilèges*.

Ravel had often wondered what he would write after the war. This work marked a beginning; but there were other things. Diaghilev approached him for another ballet. Sergey Lifar quotes a letter which Ravel wrote to Diaghilev, in which we see that he had a keen eye to the business side of things. It is of interest to quote the whole document: [4]

With reference to our conversation yesterday, I agree to compose the ballet of which you have shown me the scenario, and of which the author is the Italian poet Canguillo. This work will be finished by

[1] Biographical Sketch.
[2] *A la Gloire de Ravel*.
[3] Ibid.
[4] *La Revue musicale*, December 1938.

the end of the year (1917) so far as the piano score is concerned, and the full score by 1st April 1918.

The exclusive right of performance of this work for all countries belongs to you for the five years following the first presentation. For this work I shall receive from you the sum of ten thousand francs (10,000 fr.), payable half on the delivery of the piano score, and the rest at the delivery of the full score.

For the orchestral parts you should apply to my publisher, M. Jacques Durand.

The right of performance at concerts will rest with you until after the ballet has been performed in the town where the concert is given.

Sergey Lifar is unable to trace this work farther. He thinks, however, that although Ravel did not set the music to this par-ticular scenario, the later work *La Valse* may have been the outcome of the conversation. We shall mention that work later on.

Ravel suffered from insomnia at this time, which made ravages in his health. He returned to the sketch of the pre-war symphonic poem *Wien*, which he rechristened *La Valse: a Choreographic Poem*. Diaghilev, whether the ballet mentioned in the letter resulted in this work or not, was willing to produce it, pairing it with Stravinsky's *Pulcinella*, based on tunes by Pergolesi. Ravel set to work with keenness, as composers always do after an enforced absence from their creative activities, an absence which makes them feel that they have so much ground to make up—and this applies equally to the great and the small. On 6th January he wrote to Roland-Manuel[1]: 'I waltz frantically; I began to score it on 31st December.'

Composition was interrupted by an incident small in itself which Ravel might well have put aside with a laugh had he been in a good state of health, but which, with his nerves torn by sleep-lessness, assumed a size quite out of proportion with its importance. On 16th January 1920 the list of promotions and nominations in the order of the Legion of Honour appeared and included the name of 'M. Ravel, Joseph Maurice, composer of music.' Ravel

---

[1] Roland-Manuel, *A la Gloire de Ravel.*

always had a horror of such distinctions, and he sent off a telegram declining the honour. In his opinion to consent to be decorated implied that the state or the ruler of the state had a right to assess and judge one's work. This attitude is not unknown elsewhere, but a moment's thought proves that it is nonsense. To refuse a decoration is one thing; to make a fuss about it is another. Ravel was always so studiously courteous that we can assume that it really was his state of health which magnified an honour, made, perhaps, in good faith or possibly as the result of a joke, into an insult. Telegrams came pouring in, and he spent the day with his mind distracted from *La Valse*, which had to be finished by the end of the month.

You can imagine my despair. I have made a noise with my orchestra all day. Have you noticed that 'legionaries' resemble morphine maniacs who try everything, even deceit, to make others share their passion, perhaps to legitimize themselves in their own eyes ?

So wrote Ravel to Roland-Manuel.[1] His friends besought him to take the honour and say no more about it, but Ravel was by now riding his high horse and insisted on sending a public and official denial of his acquiescence in the affair. Honour having been thus satisfied, Ravel returned to *La Valse*. To show how far away from the original idea of *Wien* the work had progressed, the following words from the score are enlightening:

Through whirling clouds couples of waltzers are faintly distinguished. The clouds disappear gradually; a huge hall is peopled with a revolving crowd.

The first concert performance took place on 8th January 1920 at a Concert Lamoureux. The reception was enthusiastic. The critic Lindenlaub saw a Vienna of the post-war period and suggested that Ravel should go there and see how his work fitted in with what he would find. He saw in the work a species of

[1] Roland-Manuel, *A la Gloire de Ravel.*

34

danse macabre. Ravel accordingly visited Vienna towards the end of that year.

The work caused a permanent rupture between Ravel and Diaghilev. The latter refused to produce it, although, as Sergey Lifar says, the music was 'very danceable.' Ravel never forgave Diaghilev, and although the Diaghilev company formed the dancers in *L'Enfant et les sortilèges* at Monte Carlo in 1925, Ravel refused to shake hands with Diaghilev. This was behaviour to which the impresario was not accustomed, and he had serious thoughts of challenging Ravel to a duel!

La Valse is a glorious outburst of pent-up musical activity. Many see in it the last significant work of its composer and in the light of his later works consider that he wrote himself out with it.

Ravel's lines were cast in pleasant places. He now lived outside Paris, at Montfort l'Amaury, in a house called 'Le Belvédère,' surrounded by his *bibelots* and mechanical toys. His mind became distinctly whimsical. He would show his friends some Japanese ornaments, and when the friends uttered the expected cries of delight, he would inform them that the ornaments were fake. On another occasion he would point lovingly to an enormous glass bowl and when similar cries of delight were uttered again, would remark that it was only an electric light bowl. One is tempted to regard this joking as in bad taste, but on the other hand his hatred of *snobisme*, rampant all over the musical world at the time, may well have led him to malice, a malice which must have been impish, since he tried it on all his best friends. In his ultra-smart double-breasted suits he gave the lie direct to the prevailing notion that the 'artist' must necessarily be unkempt, dirty and *outré* in appearance.

'Le Belvédère' became a meeting-place for all his pupils and friends. With the splendid view from the terrace, it was ideal for parties and reunions. Ravel was a sociable fellow in most ways, although strangely withdrawn in others. His nocturnal ramblings, accentuated by his insomnia, seemed to indicate an innate loneliness, and it is well known that the person who is surrounded most of his life with friends can, at times and at root, be the loneliest creature on earth.

At this point, in the light of later events, we can see certain signs of the slowing-up of Ravel's mental processes. He was never a rapid worker, judged by standards set to-day, but everything now took longer. Although he was working at *L'Enfant et les sortilèges*, he interrupted it to attend to shorter and more pressing things. The Sonata for violin and cello, begun in 1920, was not completed until 1922, and we shall see later that he took even longer in proportion with the Sonata for violin and piano. Actually his style was changing, as does the style of most composers. With Ravel the process was slow and very deliberately mental.

All through 1920 he worked at *L'Enfant et les sortilèges*. In October he visited Vienna where he experienced the joy of recognition. Paul Stefan relates the following story: [1]

In one of the most beautiful leather shops in the town, he had chosen a portfolio: 'Mon Dieu,' he said, 'that is a good bargain; with a little foreign money in one's pocket, one can buy half the shop, in this period of inflation.' But when he asked that the portfolio might be delivered at his hotel, the shopkeeper asked if he was Ravel the composer who had written *Jeux d'eau*, because she played this piece. And when Ravel admitted it, 'Then, Maître, I will not accept any money,' she replied in perfect French. 'Accept it as a mark of my thanks for that ravishing work.'

Ravel always told this tale with relish, not so much because it touched his pride (which it did), but because he had found a shopkeeper who played *Jeux d'eau* and presented some of her goods to its composer. 'Where else can one find such a thing in these days?'

On 8th November the Swedish Ballet produced a stage version of *Le Tombeau de Couperin*; so successful was this work that Ravel himself conducted the hundredth performance on 15th June 1921.

[1] *La Revue musicale*, December 1938.

CHAPTER V

THE LAST YEARS (1922-38)

AFTER the composition of the Sonata for violin and cello Ravel took a rest and spent most of the time in entertaining his friends at 'Le Belvédère.' In the summer of 1922 Kussevitsky commissioned him to orchestrate Mussorgsky's *Pictures from an Exhibition,* work which he undertook with great joy because it kept him busy without imposing very much mental strain. A short *Berceuse on the name 'Fauré'* for violin and piano broke into the work and served to keep his creative spark alight. A concert tour followed which tired him out and did not help to cure his insomnia. Amsterdam, Venice, claimed him and he did not return to 'Le Belvédère' until the end of the year. A short stay at Saint-Jean-de-Luz, and he came over to London where he conducted *Ma Mère l'Oye* and *La Valse.*

Although *L'Enfant et les sortilèges* was still on the stocks, he decided to compose a Sonata for violin and piano. This work absorbed him completely for a time, but it progressed very slowly and was not finished until 1927. Meanwhile *L'Enfant et les sortilèges* might have been delayed indefinitely had not Raoul Gunsbourg given him a contract for production at Monte Carlo, forcing him to finish the work by the end of 1924. He concentrated for a time, but put it aside in order to compose a 'virtuosic piece in the style of a Hungarian Rhapsody' [1] for violin and orchestra, for Jelly d'Arányi. A further interruption for a short piece commissioned by *La Revue musicale, Ronsard à son âme,* and then he settled down to finish *L'Enfant et les sortilèges.*

The work was produced at the Monte Carlo Opera House in March 1925 and was an instantaneous success. The following year, on 1st February, Albert Wolff conducted the first Paris performance at the Opéra-Comique. There was no doubt about

[1] Biographical Sketch.

its success. The critics were entirely captivated, although André Messager found fault with Ravel's imitative music. The text demanded realism in the form of two cats. Messager felt that this realism was a pity, but, as Arthur Honegger pointed out, since the text required it, Ravel had no choice.

Later performances were not quite so successful and the audiences not so rapturous. Ravel's sense of humour never left him. Noticing that the occupants of a neighbouring box were whistling rather unavailingly, he sent in one of the keys from his ring to make their protest more strident.

After the success of *L'Enfant et les sortilèges* there came an offer to compose an operetta, but it came to nothing. Was this part of a curious policy which came into play in Paris about this time? As if to prove that serious composers could 'come off their perches,' some of them were commissioned to write works which were in direct contradiction to their usual manner. Vincent d'Indy was one of them, and Albert Roussel whose *Le Testament de ma tante Caroline* was something completely outside the canon.

A trip to Oslo for *L'Enfant et les sortilèges* came off in February 1926, after which Ravel returned to 'Le Belvédère' to occupy himself with the Sonata for violin and piano and another work commissioned by Mrs. Elizabeth Coolidge; this took the form of some songs with, 'if possible,' accompaniment for flute, cello and piano. He had bought a set of the complete works of Évariste Parny and immediately set his mind on the *Trois Chansons madécasses*.[1] These settings were something new for Ravel— spiteful, bitter, primitive. Ravel had made some inquiries into the elements of jazz and its origins and became attracted to its rhythmic possibilities. The Negro protests of the *Chansons madécasses* gave him opportunities. Of the three songs the most startling is undoubtedly *Aoua!* with its piercing shriek of bitterness. Jane Bathori, the heroine of the *Histoires naturelles*, tells us [2] that the flute-player Louis Fleury was driven nearly mad because

[1] Of Madagascar.
[2] *La Revue musicale*, December 1938.

of the direction to make the flute give an impression of a trombone. These settings stand out among Ravel's works not only for the origin of their musical ideas, but because 'the gentle Ravel' found within himself such a streak of bitter spitefulness. Was he himself becoming disillusioned? Did he feel within himself that his creative faculties were nearing their end or was his spiritual loneliness getting the better of him? This attraction to outside influences seems to have boded no good.

However, in 1927 he finished the Sonata for violin and piano, which he had written expressly for Hélène Jourdan-Morhange and in complete co-operation with her. It remained one of his favourite works. Early the following year he started on a tour of the U.S.A. and Canada, but just before leaving he received a commission from Ida Rubinstein to orchestrate some pieces by Albéniz. It was discovered that the sole right to make any kind of transcription of Albéniz's music was vested in the Spanish conductor Fernández Arbós. Arbós, hearing about the plan, offered to stand down, but Ravel was testy about it. 'Qu'est-ce que c'est, cet Arbós?' he asked. On thinking the matter over, he came to the conclusion that if he had to orchestrate any music, he might as well do his own. Why bother about any one else's, especially as in this particular case he would have to do it 'by kind courtesy' of someone else? We see that the 'gentle Ravel' was by now becoming very far from gentle.

However, he set off on a tour which covered as much ground as any one could possibly cover in the time. He returned on 27th April 1928, having visited New York, Chicago, San Francisco, Seattle, Vancouver, Minneapolis, New Orleans, Houston, Colorado, Buffalo, Montreal, Boston, Cambridge (Mass.) and Cleveland. We detail this tour because it will be seen that such a journey could only aggravate the mental state into which he was rapidly drifting. Needless to say the tour was a veritable triumph. Throughout he kept up a lively corre-spondence with Hélène Jourdan-Morhange.[1] 'You should see

[1] *La Revue musicale*, December 1938.

the smashing ties I have bought!' He was impressed with what he saw, but admitted to being tired out.

On his return he set to work to 'orchestrate' and the result was the *Bolero*. Much nonsense has been written about this work. Some have seen in it the final decline of Ravel's musicality. These people have never seen the ballet (we shall describe it in another chapter). Ravel himself called it a work for orchestra without music. Certainly it is original and it stands alone—and can never be repeated or copied. It was performed for the first time on 29th November by Ida Rubinstein at the Opéra.

Although Ravel had a detestation of honours when offered by his own country, he was much interested in a suggestion that he should come over here and receive the degree of D.Mus. (Oxon). The negotiations were carried out by Gordon Bryan through G. Jean-Aubry, Ravel himself declining to write any letters on the subject. Recognition from a country other than his own appealed to him at once, and he arrived in fine fettle— and in a suit the latest in cut and the most appalling in colour. Gordon Bryan has kindly furnished us with full details of this visit. This is what he says:

When in Paris during the spring of 1928, I arranged, quite light-heartedly, for an autumn visit to England by Ravel, to take part in a concert of his works at the Aeolian Hall. I little knew then what I was tackling. Although the concert itself was a real 'occasion,' with the French ambassador in the front row and a great many people unable to get in at all, we had the constant anxiety lest Ravel should somehow be mislaid *en route* and perhaps not turn up at all. He was so easily diverted from the main object in hand, and had no idea of punctuality whatever; he loved sitting indefinitely chatting after a meal, hated going to bed and equally hated getting up. Fortunately his London hostess, Madame Louise Alvar-Harding, was the soul of kindness and already knew what he was like, from participating as vocalist in his tours of North and South America, and in various European countries. Lennox Berkeley and his cousin Claude, both of them equally at home in French and English, were always on hand to prod him gently in the right direction, and between the lot of us we managed to get him to rehearsals, lunches and numerous parties, more or less on time, though it was all extremely exhausting.

He went to Oxford on 23rd October to receive the degree of D.Mus. (*honoris causa*) and was greatly interested in the details of the dignified ceremony, and incidentally in the gay pink silk robe which had to be hired for the occasion, and which he would have rejoiced to take back to Paris with him. We had quite a job to adjust its considerable length to his diminutive stature. The quizzical expression on his face while the long Latin oration was read and the anxiety with which he demanded an exact translation at the first opportunity, were typical reactions. For this ceremony his brother, who would have made two of Ravel, came over specially from France.

One of the chief pleasures of his first visit was the occasion at the Royal College of Music, when after lunch with the director, the late Sir Hugh Allen, and many of the R.C.M. notabilities the students' orchestra, conducted by Dr. (now Sir) Adrian Boult, played the second series of excerpts from *Daphnis et Chloé*. It was a magnificent performance, which we all heard from the gallery at the back, and when Ravel walked up the crowded hall, he had a tremendous ovation from the students. He appeared not to notice this, but mounted the rostrum and, instead of bowing, he bent over the score, discussing some detail of it with the conductor, and then walked back, animatedly engaged in conversation. The students were disappointed that he did not speak to them, but the only words of English that he possessed at that time were three—'one, two, pencil'—often displayed for the benefit of inquirers, and spoken with a marked American accent. He said he had been taught these with great care, when he had been conducting the American orchestras in *La Valse, Ma Mère l'Oye*, and so on.

Ravel returned for a repeat concert the following January, with a few changes in the programme.

On his return to France his health was bad. He sought the company of his friends more and more. Instead of his living quietly at 'Le Belvédère' his nocturnal ramblings round Paris became almost routine. His friend Léon Leyritz, who did the fine head in the Ravel alcove in the Paris Opéra, furnished a flat for him in the middle of Paris 'with every modern convenience.' His friends gathered round him, but he became obsessed with the fate of Chabrier, who at the end of his life could not recognize his own music.

He was full of plans, including one for an opera on Joan of Arc, and went so far as to consult Rouché about it. He also meditated upon a possible piano concerto for Marguerite Long. Suddenly there came a commission from an Austrian, Paul Wittgenstein, who had lost his right arm in the war and, being a pianist of ability and the possessor of considerable wealth, got the idea of commissioning prominent composers to write a repertory of music for him. He asked for a concerto. Immediately Ravel was fired with enthusiasm, and he found himself in the position of writing two piano concertos at the same time.

He conceived the two-handed Concerto more in the light of a *divertissement* than in that of a full-blown concerto. His admiration for Saint-Saëns's clarity had not diminished in any way. He considered Saint-Saëns's piano concertos as perfect specimens of light music, combining their deftness of touch with the spirit of Mozart (!). He considered too that the concerto should be written 'for' and not 'against' the piano, feeling that so many of the classical and standard works were too much 'in the grand manner.' Why not, therefore, write a concerto which should be gay and brilliant, not ponderous and pompous? Why not, indeed?—and with this determination he set to work.

The one-handed Concerto, conversely, should be different, although at the same time not terribly serious. This work had a chequered career. Wittgenstein did not like it and insisted on certain alterations. In 1939 Alfred Cortot, feeling that the limitations to one hand were working against its performance, brought out an edition which laid the writing out for two hands instead of one. This edition was disapproved of by Ravel's heirs, who maintained that since the composer had written it for one hand, by one hand it should be played, or not at all. Cortot pointed out that in a radio performance only those in the studio could tell how many hands were used and the objection, therefore, had no foundation. In any case, the work is written on two staves.

The two works were finished in the autumn of 1930. There was delay over the first performance of the two-handed work. Mme Long received the score on 11th November 1931, but it was not played until 14th January 1932. The other one received its first performance in Vienna on 27th November 1931.

In 1932 Ravel undertook a long tour of Europe with the two-handed Concerto, with Mme Long as the player. This proved a very tiring experience, and when Ravel was involved in a taxi accident on his return, his nervous state was unable to resist the shock, although he did not appear to have been very much hurt.

A film company decided to produce a version of *Don Quixote*, for which Ravel was commissioned to compose the musical score. The company likewise commissioned Milhaud, Ibert, Delannoy and Falla at the same time without letting them know what it was doing. Ravel composed three songs which Shaliapin would have sung. When the situation became known, and Ibert proved to be the chosen composer, Ravel instituted proceedings for indemnity to the tune of 70,000 francs. These songs, entitled *Don Quichotte à Dulcinée*, were his last compositions.

Ravel had many ideas in his head: *Shéhérazade*, his early work, a drama *Morgiana* based on the story of Ali Baba, 'full of fire and blood'(!), but these ideas came to nothing. Towards the middle of 1933 the tragedy fell upon him. He found that he was unable to write or sign his name. Later he was unable to carry out movements and gestures and appeared as if in a kind of mental stupor. The brain was refusing to function. The doctors ordered complete rest, and he went to Mont Pèlerin, near Lausanne. A tumour on the brain was diagnosed and the doctors talked learnedly about 'apraxie' and 'dysaphie.' Several treatments were tried, but to no avail. He expressed a wish to visit his beloved Spain, about which he had written so much music, and on 15th February 1935 he set off on an extended tour with Léon Leyritz.

His 'bump of locality' was, surprisingly enough, good, and

43

he was able to pilot Leyritz to all kinds of out-of-the-way places usually missed by tourists. They crossed to Morocco, and Ravel had the delightful experience of hearing a passing Moroccan whistling the *Bolero*. At Fez he was shown some wonderful native goods and works of art which the director of the Beaux-Arts suggested might well inspire him. Ravel's reply was: 'If I do anything Arabian, it will be much more Arabian than all that . . .' [1] On the return journey they visited Andalusia. Leyritz showed Ravel Seville, while Ravel showed Leyritz Córdova.

In August 1935 Leyritz joined him at Saint-Jean-de-Luz and they both set off for Bilbao, Burgos, Pamplona and Roncevaux. All this did not slow up the increasing ravages. Photos of Ravel taken at this time show a terribly sad and worried expression, not unmixed with fear—fear not of the future but of a perplexing present.

On his return he was often seen at concerts and the theatre, but he seemed in another world, completely detached from things around him. He divided his time between 'Le Belvédère,' Lavallois and Maurice Delage's. In 1937, at the Paris Festival of the Contemporary Music Society, the writer saw him at a concert of his own piano music. He seemed completely alone and unaware that it was his music which was causing the furore of enthusiasm. Later he received a tremendous ovation at one of the orchestral concerts, which was more an outburst of affection than a musical tribute. He looked as if he did not realize that it was for him that we were cheering—and an Italian composer standing next him took the honours to himself! (We were *not* cheering that Italian composer—this in case he may happen to read this book.) His blank expression was frightening.

Eventually it was decided to operate, and this was done on 19th December 1937. It left him in a state of coma, and on 28th December he quietly left us.

[1] Roland-Manuel, *A la Gloire de Ravel*.

Illness and Death

It seemed incredible that he was with us no longer. The year 1937 was a dreadful one for French music—Widor, Vierne, Pierné, Roussel and then Ravel.

He was buried in the cemetery of Lavallois, the place where he had often sought refuge in his brother's house.

CHAPTER VI

EARLY PIANO WORKS

As a rule there is no necessity to consider the earliest works of a composer with any individuality, because they have little, if any, relation to his maturity. In the case of Ravel it is necessary to look at his first published piece, the *Menuet antique* (which appeared in 1895), because in it we find figures and harmonic traits denoting the recognizable Ravel, and also because his idiom was immediately obvious, in spite of the to-be-expected influences.

The *Menuet antique* is full of faults. The writing is crowded and crabbed, and the use of the lower register of the piano is thick and ugly; however, this use of the chord of the ninth is unmistakable:

Ex. 1

avec la sourdine

The modal effect of the flattened leading-note in these two cadences anticipates the Sonatina and other works:

Ex. 2

Ex. 3

The next example is the first sign of the knack he developed in writing music calculated at first to get the hands thoroughly tied up, but which, on examination, proves to be perfectly practicable:

Ex. 4

From these seeds we can follow the logical outcome of his early instincts.

If we consider next the *Habanera*, it is because he thought it worthy of being transferred as it stood to a work of twelve years later; because it shows us his own personal harmonic inclina- tions; because it is the first musical token of his Spanish blood. In many of his later piano works we shall find a frequent use of a syncopated reiterated note, sometimes at the top, often in the middle, but very seldom in the bass. This note is used regardless of clashes; we find it in *Miroirs* and in *Gaspard de la nuit* (*Le Gibet*). This clash of sonorities is one of the chief points of interest in Ravel's maturity, and he uses it with a sure touch. His notation sometimes astonishes us with its complexity, until we discover that an alteration enharmonically of a note serves but

47

to complicate the chord still further. Thus the right hand of Example 5 staggers us momentarily until we realize that B♯ and C on the piano are not unlike one another:
Ex. 5

The next example is easier, and we accept the E♯ without hesitation:
Ex. 6

In Example 7 there is the B♯ contradicted by the high B♮ appoggiatura-wise, a device we shall find carried to a limit in *Miroirs*:
Ex. 7

In Examples 5 and 7 the rhythm of the *Habanera* is insisted on.

Gordon Bryan

D.MUS. (OXON)

Clusters of notes became one of his features, especially his use of seconds—an integral part of *Jeux d'eau*:

Ex. 8

Probably what astonishes us most is the self-assurance with which this young man of twenty formulated his style so early in life, a style so completely different from that of anything which had as yet been written. There is an amazing advance on the *Menuet antique*, written and published in the same year. In other respects, too, we find this *Habanera* important. He expressed himself naturally and instinctively in a Spanish way, having had no experience of Spain other than through his Basque blood. Manuel de Falla was greatly struck by this:

. . . a free use of rhythms, modal melodies and all the ornamental embellishments of our popular song; elements which did not alter the individual style of the composer, even though it was applied to a melodic language as distinct from that which he used in the Sonatina. . . .

But how can we explain the subtly authentic Hispanicism of our musician, knowing, on his own admission, that he had only geographical relations with our country, being born so near our frontier?

I can solve the problem quickly: the Spain of Ravel was a Spain inherited as an ideal from his mother, whose exquisite conversation, always in excellent Spanish, ravished me when she reminded me of her youth, spent in Madrid. Mme Ravel spoke of an epoch certainly before my time, but whose manners and customs had left memories which were familiar. I understood then what fascination these ever-present nostalgic memories had exercised on her son during his childhood, enhanced, doubtless, by this power which kept alive the theme of song and dance which were inseparable. And that explains the attraction Ravel felt from his earliest days for a country of which he had often dreamed; and, consequently, when he wished to characterize Spain musically, he favoured the rhythm of the habanera, the most fashionable of the songs which his mother heard in the *tertulias madrileñas* of the old days. At the same time, Pauline Viardot-García, whose high position established her with the best musicians of Paris, made this same song famous. This is how the habanera, the supreme element of all Spain, has continued to live in French music as one of our characteristics, seeing that Spain has forgotten it herself for half a century. . . .[1]

Thus blood calls to blood, instinctively. It is not surprising, therefore, that we find Ravel returning to Spanish idioms within a very few years.

The *Pavane pour une Infante défunte* (1899) may well have been suggested by some story of old Spanish church customs told him by his mother, and we can indeed imagine a stately dance round the bier placed in front of the altar. Professor Dent has a specimen of music danced by the choirboys in Seville Cathedral for the edification of the pious monks—and to the greater glory of God. Ravel contrives to give the impression of a lute by detached inner notes, the while a dignified and well-shaped tune pursues its course:

Ex. 9

The piece is in rondo form and the first episode rises high, with reiterated chords over a pedal point:

Ex. 10

At the close there is an early example of that use of block dissonances, thirteenths and ninths moving with perfect independence, which became a characteristic of Ravel and was adopted by Debussy:

Ex. 11

The second entry of the tune is widely spaced, being doubled at the fifteenth as well as the octave—another favourite device of the later Ravel.

There is enormous strength in the second episode, where a climax is reached on a dominant thirteenth:

Ex. 12

In the final entry of the tune the lute effect is doubled in semiquavers.

Roland-Manuel may speak slightingly of this piece as fit for young girls,[1] but it has a significance for the student of Ravel and for the student of piano writing. It is remarkable for its original lay-out; the tune itself requires considerable control of key, but when one thinks that he *might* have accompanied it with simple arpeggios (many composers would have done so!) and thus have turned it into a very commonplace affair, we can see the working of an original mind from the very first. It does not

[1] *A la Gloire de Ravel.*

look like piano writing, yet it comes off in performance. Further, we find much more spread in the chords; they seem, at first, impracticable, and often we are faced with clumps which need sorting out and plenty of pedal control. The closing cadence is a good example of this:

Ex. 13

The succession of thirteenths and ninths is of historical interest. In 1887 Erik Satie had written these progressions in his three *Sarabandes,* not published when Ravel first heard them:

Ex. 14

It must be remembered that Satie was the first composer to indulge in this free writing and that by 1920 it had become stereotyped enough to be the first step that students made when wanting 'to go modern.' Ravel had all the windows of freedom opened to him by this music.

Ravel said of the *Pavane* that it showed too flagrant an influence of Chabrier and that the form was poor. The former we see in the doubling of the tune at the sixteenth and octave, a device which gives it a remarkably penetrating power. As a whole, the piece may claim its ancestor in Chabrier's *Idylle*.[1] As regards form, anything more elaborate than rondo form would only have given the piece weight altogether out of proportion to itself. The orchestral version illustrates the slenderness of the fabric which is not immediately realizable when we play it on the piano.

Ravel insisted that it should be played calmly, in strict time and without any passionate or sentimental *rubato*. The English pianist Marjorie Hardwick received a lesson on this point from Ravel himself; he was most insistent. Whether it be great music or small, whether it be original and individual or pale imitation, the *Pavane pour une Infante défunte* is of the highest importance not only historically but also in respect of its composer's early declaration of style and technique.

Two years later he brought out his first work in which all the individuality in him was displayed. The *Pavane* was too small to do anything but draw attention to possibilities. *Jeux d'eau* stamped him as being a natural and instinctive writer for the piano. He himself described it as follows:

Jeux d'eau, which appeared in 1901, is the original of all the novelties in pianism which people have noted in my work.

This piece, inspired by the noise of water, and the musical sounds which fountains of water, cascades and streams make, is founded on two themes, in first-movement (sonata) form, always without subjecting itself to a classical tonal scheme.[2]

It is headed by a quotation from Henri de Régnier, 'Dieu fluvial riant de l'eau qui le chatouille.'

As might be expected, the upper register of the keyboard is exploited to the full. The principal subject is not so much a

[1] Used for the ballet *Cotillon* by the Ballets Russes de Monte Carlo and recorded by Columbia (DX 878).

[2] Biographical Sketch.

'subject' as an 'effect.' It is not an actual theme to which we can point or which we can sing:

Ex. 15

If we attempt an analysis, we may say that the subject is but six bars in length and that the connecting episode is exactly double that number. The piano writing is well spaced out but, on paper, seems to sprawl and not to lie under the hand. We shall see all through our study, however, how deceptive the 'look' of Ravel's music is.

The second subject is distinctly thematic:

Ex. 16

If the theme has no great length or continuity, it is because Ravel was not one of those who measure their tunes by so many bars; this theme is concise. Over it (or perhaps we should say through it) there is an arpeggio figure in seconds. Here we have one of those characteristics of Ravel's pianism, that of getting the fingers of each hand interlaced to the extent of fearing that they must, at some time or another, become inextricable; but how very neat is the device!

After a rattling trill and some rapid pianism formed on a broken and widely spread diatonic seventh on E♭, forming the codetta, the development section begins with a variation of the

second subject. See how deftly he shares the principal notes
between the hands:

Ex. 17

The water rises higher and higher, and with dashing *glissandi*
falls to dead level with a reference to the second subject, in fourths
—that maligned interval which did such valiant duty for composers in the 1920s:

Ex. 18

But not for long does this calm last, and the recapitulation
begins. We can hardly regard the middle section as development in the generally applied sense. Although it makes 'distinct
reference' (as the books say) to the second subject, it does little to
add anything to it, or to alter its shape. The recapitulation does
nothing but refer to the principal subject rather briefly; it then
tails off in a cadenza-like passage to the second. There is something very reposeful about this writing:

Ex. 19

The coda starts with this subject as on its first appearance, with the arpeggio seconds in groups of twelve instead of six. We go on to three staves, a favourite habit with French composers. Under a rippling added-sixth arpeggio, this placid passage

Ex. 20

leads us to the close, a tonic seventh, with hands wide apart.

Ravel was concerned mostly with the picturesque message of the movement, its symbolism. If we expect to find classical tendencies as to form, they lie only in the three-sectional lay-out. There is nothing done with the principal subject other than merely to state it. This does not necessarily mean that Ravel was 'weak in form' or that he was unable to deal with his material in the

'La Revue Musicale'

PORTRAIT BY OUVRE

expected way. We have examples contradicting this, although it cannot be said that his particular type laid any great store by it. For this we must look to the symphonic conceptions of d'Indy, Dukas, Chausson and Roussel.

Although *Jeux d'eau* was a revelation in piano sonorities and a revolution in piano technique, it has its forbear—Liszt. The idiom is quite different, but precede *Jeux d'eau* by Liszt's *Au Bord d'une source* and the parentage is obvious. Similarly, follow *Jeux d'eau* with Debussy's *Reflets dans l'eau* and the succession is established.

It is the Sonatina (1905) which has introduced Ravel to the greater number of pianists in this country, for nearly every budding pianist has studied it and learned to love its brilliancy and charm. Further, it is with this work, and with Debussy's *La Cathédrale engloutie*, that 'modern music' is usually opened to the student and the mysteries of sonorities shed their first light upon the hitherto classical vista which the student has faced. Of all Ravel's characteristic work, the Sonatina is the least difficult to play. He adheres to the classical form. If by 'sonatina' is meant something ineffably slender and slight in material and conception, then Ravel achieved perfection. We shall see that this was not to be his maturity, for, although it is an excellent introduction to him, he was not to continue indefinitely in this style; still, the girls and boys who learn it have something which sounds almost virtuosic in its small way and they can feel that they really are on the edge of 'something modern.' In addition, they get used early in their careers to the 'Ravel finger muddle.' What is more important is that they are face to face with the essence of the French spirit, of France.

The work is in three movements. The first illustrates Ravel's habit of doubling his melodies at the octave below and the later-adopted use of consecutive fifths and ninths. The principal subject is built on a succession of broken common chords—harmonically the whole movement is easy to follow and consists of no contrapuntal writing whatsoever.

Ex. 21

The second subject takes us into a world of simplicity with its open fifths in the left hand, filled in with the tenth above the root in the right hand. At its close we have an echo of the system shown in Example 1. (A similar rise and fall is one of the loveliest moments in *Daphnis et Chloé*.)

The codetta reflects the system of *Jeux d'eau*, where the left hand plays an octave passage each side of the right-hand harmony. In this way Ravel simplified a process which he developed for use in his later and larger works.

The middle section is of just the right length; one would have no less and no more. However, after the demi-semiquavers have established a sense of movement, it becomes static. The final cadence is typical Ravel of the maturity.

The Minuet which follows has all the virtues and none of the vices of the *Menuet antique*. It is described as 'Mouvement de Menuet,' by which we know that it is 'minuet type'; there is no trio. Ravel puts out his ideas exquisitely, with that neatness of harmony which was so like his personal appearance.

Here is grace and charm, with the added piquancy of a modal cadence, quasi *Menuet antique*. His key relationships sway to and fro in complete freedom; from D♭ we go straight to the tonality of F♯ with a bias towards B, but no more than a bias. Enharmonically we return to D♭, with a peregrination to C♯ minor, returning in the same way to D♭ for the cadence.

It will be noticed that although the key of the work as a whole is F♯ minor, Ravel has no compunction whatsoever about writing his middle movement in D♭ instead of C♯ major. This movement is a gem.

The finale is a *tour de force* of simple brilliancy, hard and metallic, a perfect miniature of virtuosic writing. Three bars of introduction and we are launched into sonata form with a principal subject terse and snappy, again hardly a theme:

Ex. 22

Over smooth triplet quavers, the connecting episode carries us into the second subject, breaking its progress by a return to the principal subject over a new theme of six notes.

The second subject is a version in 5–4 time of the opening theme of the first movement, presented first with moving semiquavers and then in block chords. Dashing down in block and broken common chords, the development section leads straight from a chordal sequence of A″ G″ F″ E♭″ D♭″ into a theme built largely on the notes A, G, E. There is much rushing up and down the keyboard, to no great purpose other than brilliance; the recapitulation is brought to a close rather perfunctorily.

This movement is the weakest of the three. Apart from the dazzling scurry and the effervescence of the player's technique, it has little to commend it; but, as a whole, the work is a perfect sonatina. Its slender material, its deft touch, its exquisite verve and grace all serve to make it a model of its kind. Unfortunately it is these very attributes which have given so many people the idea that Ravel was only a writer of small trifles. In the realm of the sonatina we can think of no other work which fits the limited frame so well.

Concerning the last movement of this work Mr. Gordon Bryan gives us some enlightening information:

The Sonatina for piano was published by Durand in 1905, and up to 1928 two accidentals were missing in the last movement—bars 13 and 15, where there should be sharps before the D's in the bass. (Note that when the figure returns shortly in another key, the G's are already in the key-signature.) Ravel was disgusted beyond measure when I pointed this out to him and immediately sat down to write a letter to Messrs. Durand which by now must have burnt a hole in their files. He alluded to this several times later, with a satisfied grin, and it appealed to his sense of humour that he should have to come to England to be told of this *horreur*.

Reader, will you please check on your own copy?

Let us for a moment examine what we have seen. At first glance there is nothing of importance except *Jeux d'eau*, if we are thinking of the music by itself, as music. However, as long as we realize that these are early works and hardly to be considered as more than 'pieces,' we can put them in the right perspective, for they have their significance in the natural order of the develop-ment of the Ravel genius. Certainly there is nothing big or broad, nothing in the grand manner; perhaps it is their very slenderness which makes us feel that they are of little moment. There are, however, several points we must observe. In the first place we have found certain bases, harmonic and personal. The establishment of the former so early in a career is remarkable and we can think of few composers whose early pieces sound so like their mature ones; even the *Pavane* is unmistakable. The free use of dissonances, the subtle rhythms, the novelty of the pianism, the use of the piano for picturesque purposes—all these are features which he developed so individually. His personality creeps in everywhere, his dapper self, and his Spanish blood which inspired him with all its characteristic elements.

It will be seen that the progress was rapid.

CHAPTER VII

LATER PIANO WORKS

THE set of five pieces entitled *Miroirs* marks the establishment of Ravel's firmness of style and pianism. Here he succeeds in doing more than use the piano as a medium for pianistic ideas, as in the Sonatina; he brings it into line with the orchestra as an illustrator of programme or descriptive music. In all this achievement he shows his consummate craftsmanship of technique and his natural bent as a writer for the piano. There are few composers whose instincts have been so sure.

His thoughts flowed naturally and we feel that no other medium will do—although he himself orchestrated some of the piano pieces. Conversely, as we shall see, his orchestral works transfer well to the piano.

In *Miroirs* we find Ravel's characteristics in full. His pianism is wider in scope and variety than in *Jeux d'eau* or the Sonatina and increases correspondingly with his harmonic range. Not all the *Miroirs* are of equal interest, but all display the same wide outlook and contrast; from the clashing harmonies and syncopated pedal in *Noctuelles* and *Oiseaux tristes*, the widespread arpeggios in *Une Barque sur l'océan*, the brittle, percussive effects in *Alborada del gracioso*, to the exploitation of sonorities in *La Vallée des cloches* we can find the whole Ravel canon (a canon which was to reach its widest scope in *Gaspard de la nuit* [1908]), without which there would have been no Debussy *Préludes*. Debussy never ran risks which Ravel took in his stride.

Each *Miroir* is dedicated to a brother-Apache. The first, *Noctuelles* (to Léon Paul Fargue), is not very appealing musically, although it contains some musical interest. It abounds in 'Ravellianisms' such as these:

Ex. 23

(The last bar develops from the Sonatina.)

Ex. 24

(Here we see an adoption of the syncopated figure.)

Ex. 25

(An unblushing use of common chords.)

Generally speaking, *Noctuelles* amounts to very little from the listener's point of view, but the player finds every bar a joy.

Oiseaux tristes (to Ricardo Viñes) is a different matter. Here Ravel is concerned with an expression of feeling. The caged birds are sad and restricted. A plaintive melody, a quiet dignity as the birds sit on their perches—and then the frantic fluttering of wings against the side of the cage. The contradiction of sharp and natural, an appoggiatura effect, is used to the full and, again, common chords are the foundation:

Ex. 26

Une Barque sur l'océan (to Paul Sordes) gives us a picture of a sunlit Mediterranean, in the afternoon; there is a breeze which ripples up the blue water. This is 'liquid' music of a different order from *Jeux d'eau* and of considerably less invention: indeed, the arpeggio writing smacks slightly of the commonplace—but it comes off. A certain strength asserts itself as the sea shows signs of rising and the craft rides before the wind.

Ex. 27

It goes on for a long time. Of all Ravel's pieces one may say that the writing in this work lies most readily under the hand accustomed to the Liszt tradition. It is some distance from that composer in point of harmonic thought, however.

Alborada del gracioso (to M. D. Calvocoressi) is outstanding, and Ravel here is on the fringes of Spain. The title is difficult to translate—literally *Dawn Song (Aubade) of the Buffoon*—but there is no doubt as to its musical meaning. If ever there was a demonstration of debauchery in music this is it. Ravel 'zipps off' with twanging guitars and clacking castanets, all conspiring in typical rhythms. In the middle we reach that moment when the buffoon seems 'to wish he hadn't done it' and the music calms down gratefully; but soon the twanging and clacking recommence and the piece riots to a glorious close.

This is something terrific in piano writing—it is equally terrific in its orchestral form! The instrument is used percussively; of thematic material there is very little, and it is impossible to call to mind more than a mere fragment. The technique is widened by *glissandi* in thirds and fourths. This is music which comes dangerously near to being merely 'effective,' but it is saved by the genuineness of its rhythms and melodies.

La Vallée des cloches (to Maurice Delage) is, with *Oiseaux tristes*, the most successful of the set—*Alborada* seems rather out of the picture. In this, the last of the *Miroirs*, Ravel experiments with sonorities, not with clashes or clusters of notes, but with single tones which ring out above the chiaroscuro. The bells are illustrated with perfect fourths:

Ex. 28

Later they clang softly beneath an octave melody:

Ex. 29

Miroirs are a notable contribution to piano literature. They freed the piano itself from its traditional shackles and made it an instrument of poetry. They were contemporary with Debussy's first series of *Images* and preceded the first book of *Préludes* by five years. *Reflets dans l'eau*, as we have seen, traces back to *Jeux d'eau*.

It is not always a 'safe bet' when composers who normally 'think big' come down to earth to write music of a simple nature either for children to play or to illustrate some childish subject. In the first place they usually fail to reduce their thoughts and technique to the proper level of simplicity; in the second there is a tendency to put too much weight on the subject or to descend to depths of the most appalling banality. It was Ravel's passion for *bibelots* which helped him in the composition of *Ma Mère l'Oye*.

The actual inspiration was drawn from the illustrations to a book, illustrations rather in the style of our Arthur Rackham. It is a pity that he did not make more use of the piano duet form, for this suite of fairy-tales shows his technique to have been admirable from this point of view.

Here is no pianism, and we may wonder if perhaps he sub-consciously projected his thoughts orchestrally. Certainly the last piece, *The Fairy Garden awakes*, suggests this because of its chordal writing: it is almost organ music! Ravel's imagination was fully alive to fantasy in each of the movements, and his inherent Spanishness comes out even in a fairy-tale.

The first movement, *Pavan of the Sleeping Beauty*, does not remind us of the early *Pavane pour une Infante défunte*, and it is refreshing to find a composer who does not repeat himself when writing twice in the same form. It is but twenty bars long and, except for three chromatic notes, diatonic throughout. We find even in this miniature certain features which we have come to recognize—in this case it is a little repeated D which rings out softly. With what charm and dignity do the courtiers dance their stately pavan round the bed of the sleeping child!

The extreme neatness with which Ravel answers his first phrase, rising while another falls, a device (if you like) which with certain other composers would look like mathematical precision, has been likened to his trim self.

The second movement, *Petit Poucet* or *Hop-o'-my-Thumb*, is headed by a quotation from the story by Perrault:

He thought that he could easily find his way back by means of the bread-crumbs which he had dropped along the path; but he was very much surprised when he was unable to find a single crumb: the birds had eaten them all up.

The wandering Hop-o'-my-Thumb, full of anxiety and childish fears, is drawn by a continuous moving figure in thirds. Beginning with two beats in a bar, each bar adds one beat until we reach five: thus we get a charming effect of doubt and trouble. The child moves all over the place, trying to find the track. Melodically, we have a charming tune, as diatonic as one could wish:

Ex. 30

The direct descendant of this diatonic line-drawing is found in *Daphnis et Chloé*, at the 'Dawn of Day' episode.

Hop-o'-my-Thumb grows panic-stricken, and the intensity of his fear reminds us of the characteristic so much exploited in the *Introduction and Allegro* and the string Quartet, where the melody is doubled at the octave in the extreme parts. The saucy chirrup of the birds is an obvious orchestral effect, but this need not blind us to the charm of the music as music. Hop-o'-my-Thumb is left, at the end of the piece, standing baffled.

If Ravel took his Sleeping Beauty to Spain, he next ran off to the Orient where 'Laideronnette, Empress of the Pagodas,' is taking her bath in the garden. The story, from *Le Serpent en vert* by Mme d'Aulnoy, tells us that the moment the empress stepped into her bath the air was filled with the sounds of tinkling bells and little 'theorboes.'

This is almost a study on the black keys, for the treble player uses no others; the bass is more venturesome. The exquisite charm and daintiness of this writing leaves us delighted and fascinated. There is no mistaking the personality behind this music. It may be said that it does not take a great brain to fool about on the black keys of the piano, that any schoolboy can do it with his fists—and does. But does the schoolboy hit upon

this succession of notes, so satisfactory in themselves, regardless of
their foundation?

Ex. 31

No doubt this can be explained in terms of five-note scales,
etc., but let us have done with this nonsense in such a simple
connection and talk about the black keys of the piano. It is
this type of thought, together with his personality and attraction
to all things minute which has earned Ravel the title of 'a small
master,' an absurd assessment—as though one were to say the same
of Beethoven because of his Bagatelles and Sonatinas or of
Schubert because of his Viennese waltzes!

The fourth movement, *Beauty and the Beast*, is the most obviously
imaginative of the suite. It is the least satisfactory for this reason.
One expects the Beast to growl deep down in the bass and
Beauty to be characterized by a graceful waltz movement; also,
the transformation to be illustrated by a harp *glissando*. The
waltz movement in itself is charming, and it must be admitted
that the rumblings of the Beast are necessary for the story.

The suite ends with an impressive movement as the Fairy
Garden wakes up. The charming four-part writing gives us a
convincing picture of the peaceful atmosphere, while the little

tolling bell which comes to life adds reality to an unreal scene.
Again, the diatonicism of the piece is striking.

To be able to come down to earth on this level is sometimes
considered a sign of greatness, for it is only the great who can be
small and, at the same time, preserve their personality. *Ma Mère
l'Oye* cannot be classed as great music, and no one could ever
consider doing so; but there is room in the world for exquisite
things as well as for magnificent creations. The trouble is that
there are few which really are exquisite; most are banal and
vapid. This suite stands almost alone.

Ravel added a prelude and interludes when it was used as a
ballet in 1912.

In the same year as this miniature Ravel produced *Gaspard
de la nuit*, one of the greatest works in the realms of romantic
and symbolistic music, a work in which the piano is exploited
to its utmost limits—but still remaining practical and practicable. Yet he would be the last to have maintained that it
was in any way experimental; on the contrary, it is the logical
result of *Miroirs*.

If pianists complain of the technical difficulties of *Miroirs*, they
have harder ground to break in *Gaspard de la nuit*, but these
difficulties have greater rewards.

Gaspard de le nuit is advisedly virtuoso music, but with the
addition of a musical content that was the *raison d'être* for the whole
work. Balakirev's *Islamey* and other such virtuosic pieces are
concerned first and foremost with the performer's technique;
Gaspard makes it subservient to the musical thought and subject.
It is strange that other composers have not followed this idea.
Elaborate works for piano which have a programmatic basis are
few and far between. Either the technique is so far in advance
of the musical content as to make musicians lose all interest in
the work as music, or else the subject is too heavy for the music;
in both cases there is no balance of interest. Ravel set an example
which has not yet been followed, despite the thousands of things
written for piano for individual players and as a bait for the great

to undertake them. Ravel proved his greatness in this *genre*; that his few ventures in the realm of the short piece are failures does not in any way detract from this greatness. It has been said that Chopin was not a great composer because he wrote solely for the piano. This is false. It is not the matter, but the manner which points to greatness. Pianists have reason to be grateful to many composers for providing them with material of value. Rakh-maninov, Skriabin and Ravel are cases in point. That they ignore the second, overplay a few of the works of the first and con-fine themselves to two or three of the third is no reflection on the composers. It is lamentable that we hear the complete work of *Gaspard de la nuit* so rarely, because we shall see that it uses the resources of the piano to their fullest and carries on the Liszt tradition to its zenith. In this work pianists have not only oppor-tunities for showing themselves off but the additional advantage of interpretative possibilities, these requiring considerable mental concentration. However, such lamentations get us nowhere. Here is the work and no amount of persuasion seems to avail.

Between the fantasy of Perrault and the magic of Louis Bertrand lies the path from white to black magic.[1] Both are fantastic, but whereas Perrault was concerned with children's fairy-tales, Bertrand deals with serious things.

Gaspard de la nuit is in three parts: 'Ondine,' 'Le Gibet' and 'Scarbo.' Each has a programme. In the first we have the traditional story of a beautiful spirit seducing handsome young men to their watery death by the beauty of her song and appearance; the second gives us a graphic picture of a gibbet swaying in the wind on a desolate moor; the third draws a fantastic figure which seems to beggar actual description, a figure from the nether regions, evil, 'infernal.' Many composers would have gone to the orchestra with such themes. We have seen that so many of Ravel's piano works score well for orchestra. Such is the pianism, the essential pianism of this work, that neither he nor

[1] *A la Gloire de Ravel.*

any one else has ever attempted to transcribe it, even though *Le Gibet* offers considerable possibilities.

The virtuosity requires, in *Ondine*, nimble finger dexterity. It is doubtful if a really accurate performance of the opening reiterated figure is given in one case in twenty. The repetitions have to be exact and at the proper pace—which is faster than it looks—the technique has to be perfect. It also demands the ability to sweep widely spaced arpeggios smoothly and without a break. Nevertheless, this is the one movement which is played with any frequency.

The sprite sings her seductive song in what we can see to be a typical Ravel *cantabile*, diatonic, rhythmic and smooth—another refutation of the charge of short-windedness.

Ex. 32

(Note a rhythm which anticipates *Daphnis et Chloé*.) This theme gets itself on each side of the right hand in the usual Ravel manner, so baffling at first sight, yet so pianistic on examination—a true extension and expansion of *Jeux d'eau* and the Sonatina. We hear the sounds of little waterfalls and rivulets enticing the stranger as Ondine sits on her rock, combing her hair and singing seductively. All through the movement we experience a hard feeling, heartless and cold, a kind of fatalistic atmosphere as of one victim being no more or less than routine in a day's life. While nature seems to have set herself to be beautiful, the ugly spirit of Ondine makes use of beauty for cruel purposes. The whole work is surprisingly cruel in conception. From the musician's point of view 'there is much to admire' (as a well-known critic would say) in the way Ravel treats the obvious and makes it significant—see the arpeggio figures which a lesser composer would have made commonplace. The decoration is masterly and never obscure.

Le Gibet demands technique which is apparent to the player and not to the listener. In Ondine the listener can hear the difficulties the player is facing. In Le Gibet the difficulties lie inside the music, in the manipulation of the harmonies. Thus there is no display of any kind.

Ravel's fondness for pedal-points is exemplified in Le Gibet, although in this case the pedal-point is thematic and has a purpose. The gibbet with its clanking chains sways in the wind. This syncopated B♭ continues inside the harmonies, which paint a picture of desolation and tragedy. An extreme use of common chords in their root positions points to the real simplicity of Ravel's harmonic thought. One can think of only one other modern composer whose mastery of the common chord is so complete—Ralph Vaughan Williams, himself a pupil for a short while of Ravel. This admirable piece of tone-painting is the shortest of the three movements, and the most moving because it is the most human. Ondine and Scarbo are creatures of fancy, and although men do not hang in gibbets nowadays in desolate places and blasted oaks are not used for hanging purposes, we have read enough to know this as an actuality and a reality of life which was, at one time, positive.

There is a clearly marked melodic line throughout the work, a line curiously restricted in range but which portrays excellently the feeling of solitude and desolation. The music moves us strangely in its fullness. Of the three movements, Le Gibet is the least spectacular and the least difficult technically. Perhaps it is its gruesomeness which does not commend it to players.

Scarbo, equally macabre, transcends the other two movements in technical requirements. Prefaced to the music is a quotation which gives us the clue to the work:

Oh! the times I have heard and seen him—Scarbo, when at midnight the moon shines in the heavens like a silver crown on a blue banner emblazoned with golden bees.

73

The times I have heard his laugh sounding in the shadow of my alcove, and his claws grating on the silk of my bed curtains.

The times I have seen him jump on to the floor, pirouette on one foot and revolve round the room like the fallen spindle of a sorceress's distaff.

Did I believe that he vanished? The dwarf grew tall between the moon and myself like the belfry of a Gothic cathedral, a golden bell swinging on its pointed tip.

But soon his body faded, diaphanous as the wax of a candle, his face grown pale as the wax of a candle end—and suddenly he disappeared.

Another short quotation, from Hoffmann's *Nachtstücke*, gives us further light:

He looked under the bed, up the chimney, in the chest—nobody. He could not understand where he got in, or where he escaped.

These quotations do not give us any definite picture of this diabolic image, and image it must remain, each one forming his own picture. That Scarbo was a creature of nightmare fantasy is apparent.

Scarbo is vicious music. It scratches as its namesake might scratch on the windows and curtains. M. Gil-Marchex [1] suggests that the opening figure of the theme could be applied to words which illustrate the state of mind of one who hears the demon but cannot see him:

Ex. 33

Quelle hor-reur!

This is fanciful but sensible, and even if Ravel did not think of it himself, it gives the key to the work. There is nothing diatonic about this music. Ravel indulges all his resources of chromatic harmony and pianism to the full. His fondness for major seconds is given full vent and the percussive outlook on the piano is developed as far as possible. Of theme there is very little save the few bars with which the work opens after its snappy and scratchy introduction. It is not impressionism in any way but verges

[1] *La Revue musicale*, December 1938.

almost on the bounds of realism. We can see this imaginary figure—of course each one sees its shape according to his own imagination. It is one of the masterpieces of virtuosic music, and of music itself. The piano's capabilities seem to be exhausted. Here the player can indeed shine, but at a cost of much hard work. Nevertheless, with all its difficulties, the music is magnificently laid under the hands. There is no hesitation from the point of view of continuity. The pianism may perhaps anticipate that of the Toccata in *Le Tombeau de Couperin*, a work, as will be seen, very far removed from this one. When we consider that *Scarbo* was composed in 1908, we can find the measure of Ravel's stature among composers.

As we have said, *Le Gibet* and *Scarbo* are not very often performed. Many pianists play at *Ondine*; few play it.

The year 1909 was indeed sterile for Ravel. The only thing he seems to have written is the *Minuet on the name 'Haydn,'* a piece which fails singularly to hold the balance between simplicity and complication. An explanation of the method of writing a piece on the letters of Haydn's name may perhaps make plain a problem which French composers have often set the world. It is accomplished simply by renaming the notes of the theme or the scale in rising octaves. There is, of course, no reason save custom for calling the note C by this letter—indeed we have the German variant which gives us H for B♮. If one chooses to call a note 'N' and provided due notice is given, who shall gainsay it? This kind of thing was done in some little pieces by Honegger, Poulenc and Ibert written in honour of Roussel. It may not be convincing, but it is a delightful idea. French composers have for years been in the habit of contributing short pieces to do honour to certain great names. *La Revue musicale* produced several numbers of these *hommages* to Ronsard, Dukas, Bach, Fauré, Debussy and, as mentioned above, Roussel. These pieces are intended not so much for performance as for tangible tributes. It is a charming scheme and it would be interesting to hear them. The only examples of this kind of tribute we have in England are *The*

Triumphs of Oriana in honour of Queen Elizabeth I, a similar set of madrigals in honour of Queen Victoria, *A Little Organ Book* in honour of Parry, a set of dedicatory pieces by Herbert Howells entitled *Lambert's Clavichord* and a collection of Bach transcriptions for Miss Harriet Cohen. Unpublished as a whole is a set of orchestral pieces by pupils of Vaughan Williams.

Ravel's Minuet is negligible. It does not keep to the opening simplicity and on the second page becomes involved and overladen. He was not happy in the occasional piece and in this instance is dull and meaningless.

We have already read of the scandal of the *Valses nobles et sentimentales*. Compared with *Gaspard de la nuit*, these are small fry for both performer and listener, but what can be absorbed and can pass unnoticed in a virtuoso work loses its disguise in plain and straightforward writing, unadorned by figuration. The *Valses nobles et sentimentales* seem plain sailing to-day; what was it that caused the riot in 1911?

First, we may put part of it down to the unexpected nature or the work. Might not an audience be prepared by the title 'Valses' to expect the Viennese variety, with its clear melodic line and 'pom-pom' accompaniment? To those in that frame of mind the very first bar must have given it a jolt. Add to this the exasperation of the composer's anonymity, and it will be seen that the omens were all set for disaster.

Secondly, the brutality of the square harmonies with which the work opens must have seemed a mere succession of splashes ('any note will do'), and the conflicting rhythms and unusual use of the piano, especially at the end, would make the thought seem orchestral rather than pianistic; and the music changing its clean-cut lines for what we may rather loosely term 'impressionism' must have struck too new a note.

The work is worthy of close attention, for it is a landmark not only in Ravel's output but in the course of the progress of French music to freedom and individuality. Ravel himself regarded it affectionately, including the seventh waltz among what he considered his representative works. The motto of the *Valses nobles et sentimentales* is a quotation from Henri de Régnier—the second work to be suggested by this poet—'Le plaisir délicieux et toujours nouveau d'une occupation inutile.'

The opening waltz sets us off with bold chordal writing, full of sway and swing (in the right sense of the word). There is nothing obscure here, and the composer determined to let the sound speak for itself. For the first time we see here a process. Anything of this nature was foreign to Ravel. He had no systems, no 'isms' (we except his Hispanicism as being a characteristic innate in him which came to the surface only when dealing with Spanish subjects). On the third page there are the following bass progressions:

Ex. 34

Ravel was not to use any other kind of system or process for many years to come.

The second waltz is gracious and charming. After a very chromatic introduction, he draws a chaste, diatonic melody, with distinct modal atmosphere, a type of melody of which he was very fond, and which he brought to complete development in *Le Tombeau de Couperin* (the Minuet):

Ex. 35

This gentle tune becomes involved towards the end in the chromatic meshes of the opening, but it in no way loses its personality, and the balance between the two thoughts is carefully measured and does not in any way sound incongruous.

Waltz No. 3 moves quickly, again very diatonically with a constant use of added-sixth chords in the right hand. In contrast, the fourth and fifth waltzes have a chromaticism which would be cloying were it not that the movements are short. Once more he resorts to a process, and the bass in two places in No. 5 moves in leaps of the perfect fifth.

No. 6, like No. 3, covers the ground quickly, rising up and up—although he does not hesitate to use the lower registers of the piano, with both hands.

The seventh waltz (his favourite) is the longest of the set. In it we find clear ternary form, the middle section having a notable change of rhythm. The opening section is graceful and rather happy. The middle section gives the right-hand melody in two-in-a-bar, with the accompaniment in three; this has a shifting and uncertain effect which is considerably enhanced when the first section makes its return in the original triple time. This 'change of diaeresis,' as it is called, relieves the heavy *one*, two, three of waltz music.

The eighth and last waltz, in the nature of an epilogue, is impressionistic in outlook. The harmonies are full and we revel in the bath of misty sound. Instead of the traditional triumphant coda the work ends with three bars *ppp, en se perdant* (implying that they are to be quite soft!).

This is one of Ravel's most successful works. He set out to provide contrast with *Gaspard de le nuit*, to write a music clear, clean and stark in outline. He fulfils this ambition in no uncertain measure. There is nothing obscure or mushy about the work. Everything is easy to follow and above-board. The orchestral version will be referred to later, in the chapter on his orchestration.

We pass over a short *Prélude* written in 1913 and two parodies

in *A la manière de . . .* of Borodin and Chabrier. Ravel colla-
borated with Alfredo Casella only in the second book of this
work, to which the latter contributed parodies of d'Indy and
Ravel, neither of which is very good. Ravel has certainly caught
the mood and spirit of a Borodin waltz, but it is too much of an
actual imitation. Why he parodied Chabrier by means of a
paraphrase of a song from Gounod's *Faust* is a question which
he alone could have answered. These pieces are utterly useless.
They are not even funny.

It was after his demobilization in 1917 that he finished the
composition of what was to have been a *Suite française*. It finally
came to light in a suite *Le Tombeau de Couperin* and each movement is dedicated to a friend killed in the war. Ravel did not
attempt to write music in the style of Couperin, but satisfied himself with framing the movements of his suite within the limits of
the suites of the period, with titles such as Couperin and the other
early French composers might have used. This was the last
considerable work for piano solo he wrote.

The movements in question are *Prélude, Fugue, Forlane, Rigaudon,
Menuet* and *Toccata*. The *Prélude* justifies its title both as a
prelude to the suite and as a prelude in construction—a piece built
on one figure, in this case triplets of semiquavers. The music
moves along continuously with no great emphasis on theme.
What actual theme there is lies hidden for the most part in the
pianism which is of the brilliant order, virtuosic enough to
satisfy the demands of both those with technique of the first order
and those with a certain limitation in this direction. The
music lies well under the hands and is of an extreme harmonic
simplicity.

The *Fugue* is not particularly interesting. Never once does its
range go below second line in the bass, and then it is only a pedal-
point. For the rest, both hands are in the treble clef throughout
and the general atmosphere is one of calm and placidity. The
part-writing is clear and lucid, but one feels that it lacks the
necessary impulse; did he write it in a disinterested spirit?

The *Forlane* is a kind of jig, of ancient Italian origin. Unlike the gigues generally known in the suites of Bach, it is not contra-puntal or *fugato* in form. Indeed, it is far removed from these elements and one must realize that the comparison with the gigue is only in the spirit, which is very bright and happy. Actually, this particular *Forlane* is on the plaintive side. The charming little opening theme almost hurts by its sharpness:

Ex. 36

It has been described as suggesting the taste of pine-apple, 'a pleasure bordering on pain,' as Lamb says in his *Essay on Roast Pig*. It is music of the clavecin order translated into terms of the ordinary piano.

The *Rigaudon* is the most popular number in the suite. Its diatonic strength, thoroughly masculine and breezy, its brilliancy of chordal opening, and its sudden change to chromatic sweetness and brittleness, together with the bracing effect of the whole atmosphere on both performer and listener, have combined to bring it into relief against the other movements—this movement and the preceding *Forlane* make an excellent pair. The gentle middle section is usually taken much too slowly and consequently flops and sags. Ravel marked it *moins vif*, but this does not mean the *andante ma non troppo* in which pianists usually play it. It is piquant music, and without the tang of piquancy it loses all its vitality. Ravel revels in diatonic discords. Much of it may be said to be of the nature of Debussy's early suites, but Debussy never had the drive which Ravel displays in this music.

The following *Menuet* takes us to a realm of such simplicity that one wonders at the paring down of the composer's natural technique. We find an echo of the *Menuet antique* and the Sonatina in the modal cadence, with the flattened leading-note. The 'Musette' (taking the place of the usual trio) reminds us of a tune in *Valses nobles et sentimentales* (Ex. 35). This time the tune is harmonized throughout in block common chords over a pedal-point. Like its parallel it, too, gets involved in the opposite nature of the main theme, a theme in itself, be it noted, out of the picture only in point of mode. An original cadence gives us a double inner trill.

The final *Toccata* is distinguished by a technical demand far exceeding that of any of the other movements. It is a virtuosic *tour de force* of no great thematic significance (like the opening prelude) but of a brittleness thoroughly characteristic of a modern composer's outlook on the percussive side of the piano, which, after all, has been the basis of toccatas ever since the form was first devised.

This suite is beautifully clear and pure. There is no attempt at impressionism. It is pure pianism throughout, written in an abstract frame of mind. Perhaps this kind of suite, in the spirit of the old clavecinists, gives us the kind of music they themselves would have written had they had the present harmonic resources. If this is the case, Ravel would seem to have caught just that spirit. There are works one would like to have written oneself; this is one of them.

There was to be no other large-scale work for piano solo. In 1919 Ravel composed a *Frontispice* for piano duet for a book by Canudo, *Poème du Vadar*, published in the *Feuillets d'Art* series. This little piece is unknown to most pianists and appears to be unprocurable now. In 1927 he contributed a tiny *Fanfare* to the omnibus ballet *L'Éventail de Jeanne*, for which the music was written by nine other composers in addition to Ravel. This does nothing more or less than carry out its intention as a heralding of the rise of the curtain and would be quite unsuitable for performance on its own. Originally this work was performed with

Ravel

piano; later it was scored, and its dainty music, devised for performance in a room, was quite lost on a full-size stage.

Taking all the points of Ravel's piano music into consideration, as we have done, it will be instructive to read a pianist's view of them. Mr. Myers Foggin has kindly sent the following opinion, formed on his own experience:

When a pianist studies Ravel's music he is always well repaid for the many hours he practises, for, apart from its value as music, it is so well written for the instrument that it can, with a reasonable technique, be not only played but also controlled. At times it is very difficult, and at other times the hands do tend to get in one another's way (thanks to the influence of the two keyboards of the clavecin), but there can be no doubt that Ravel's knowledge of the capabilities of the instrument and of pianoforte technique was vast.

The interpretative artist is faced with so many problems that it would seem invidious to mention any particular essentials in the interpretation of any piano music, but certain requisites do present themselves in the studying of Ravel's music. The pianist is constantly aware of the necessity of observing carefully the composer's meticulous editing (particularly with regard to the note-lengths and phrasing), of balancing the sounds so that they are perfectly proportioned to one another, and of pedalling in such a way that the harmonic texture is maintained.

This confirms what we have discovered, and thus we complete a survey of Ravel's contribution to the piano repertory.

CHAPTER VIII

THE CONCERTOS

THAT Ravel never wrote a full-length concerto for any instrument save the piano is surprising, for he had at his disposal all the most eminent instrumentalists of his time. Since it was scored for violin and orchestra, we must mention the *Tzigane* which he wrote for Jelly d'Arányi in 1924; but although it requires virtuosic capabilities on the part of the player, it is not a concerto.

Composers sometimes seem uncomfortable outside their immediate surroundings. No doubt to connect a Hungarian violinist and Hungary is thoroughly logical, and no doubt to write a work *à la hongroise* is not the hardest task a composer can set himself, but Ravel does not seem at home in the fields and plains of Hungary. Recently what in our innocence we imagined to be Hungarian folk and traditional music has been exposed in no uncertain manner both in print and on the radio. It seems likely, therefore, that we shall have to re-orientate our ideas in this direction. However, Ravel decided that music of a quasi-gypsy type was the most suitable for Miss d'Arányi, and the *Tzigane* is true to type, but of course far in advance of the understanding of an ordinary gypsy player. We are reminded of his remark that if he ever wrote anything Arabian it would be more Arabian than anything he had heard of the genuine article. In *Tzigane* he attempted to get inside the melancholy of the Puszta nomad. That he succeeded cannot be in doubt, but that the task was congenial cannot be conceded. The essence of the music was not in his make-up, and the result is a kind of pastiche which hovers very nearly on the edge of the commonplace.

We may say, therefore, that the *Tzigane* supplied a required article, that so far as the player is concerned, it satisfies every need; but, so far as the Ravel canon is concerned, it is a work over which we would pass, without haste but without pause. It is certainly amazingly effective music; but this in itself constitutes no virtue, for the world teems with effective music, with music which comes off but in actual fact says very little, if anything at all. Violinists will continue to play *Tzigane* because it is so well written for the violin and the composer's name is, after all, Ravel. Musicians will continue to listen to it as a piece of virtuoso writing, but in no other light.

It was some years later that the idea of a concerto in any form occurred to him, and then he found himself writing two at once. It would be hard to find two such divergent works of the same kind in any composer's output. The Concerto for two hands is light, breezy and in the style of a divertimento; that for the left hand is full of dignity, colour and opulence, with no concessions to the listener's repose of mind. The first is frothy, the second very much in the grand manner—not, be it noted, the grand manner of Tchaikovsky, Rakhmaninov or Richard Strauss, but in a manner grand in conception, style and theme. It interested Ravel to be so occupied, and the moving spirits behind the works gave him the necessary urge—Marguerite Long, a Frenchwoman of grace and charm; Paul Wittgenstein, an Austrian maimed in the 1914-19 war, serious-minded and brave in the overcoming of a disability. Finger dexterity as opposed to strength; feminine music against masculine; ebullience of spirits alongside dignity. It is impossible to say that one is more successful than the other. Each in its way is complete, but we feel we should like more of the one-handed work.

The two-handed work, henceforth to be called here the Concerto in G major, is brilliant and brittle, a *tour de force* in the truest sense. If the pianist is to be a virtuoso, so is the trumpet player in the orchestra, and few are capable of tackling the opening movement with any confidence. Unfortunately, it is a movement which depends on its speed. A radio performance once gave us an interpretation of enormous dignity and portentousness, but it was not clear whether the difficulties lay with the trumpet player or the pianist. Taken below speed, the whole thing

Durand et Cie

MAURICE RAVEL (1914)

sounds absurd. Taken up to speed, there must be few who can
resist its appeal. It is in first-movement form. Ravel requires
a harp as well as the ordinary concerto orchestra. For this
instrument he interpolates a section which is out of the picture
and sounds far too much like a 'fill-up.'

He displayed considerable ingenuity in the cadenza, and this
is the case also with the Concerto in D major (that for one hand).
The cadenza of the G major is unique with its right-hand trills
over the arpeggio left hand, a process known to Liszt, of course,
and regarded in the same way by Ravel. True, the right hand
trills away over the chordal theme in several concertos, but in
the Ravel the trills seem almost thematic, whereas in the others
(e.g. in Grieg's) they are only incidental. Pianists who cannot
enjoy playing the piano or enjoy music for itself would be advised
to avoid this work. Those who are able to do both will find the
rhythm delightful, percussive and concise, yet never 'jazzy.'

The slow movement is unique because of its extreme simplicity.
If there was show in the first movement, there is certainly none in
the second. Indeed, the tune is so plain, so unadorned, that
pianists might well scorn it. Although the time signature is 3–4,
the left hand throughout is in 6–8, and this gives the music a
peaceful and rocking effect. For some bars the pianist plays
simple common chords with the left hand while the right is
occupied with the tune, entirely unelaborated and extraordinarily
diatonic. At the close of this incident we get a flute entry which
only a French genius could have written, something so exquisitely
tender and polished, so chaste and smooth:

Ex. 37

The placidity of the thought continues and even when the orchestra has the tune under trickling scale passages there is never any feeling of violence or passion. At the end we hear a kind of echo of the flute entry quoted above, a charming effect not usually attained with such simplicity in a concerto:

Ex. 38

The third movement is high-spirited indeed. If Ravel intended to write light music, he has given us a model here. The pianism is again percussive, with its repeated semiquavers. It is in this movement that we find a certain point of similarity with the other Concerto. A descending figure of three notes in the work under discussion gives a feeling akin to skittishness, whereas in the other it adds a portentous and ominous feeling to an already highly charged atmosphere. It is strange that the same three notes can sound so different in two contexts:

Ex. 39 'A'   'B'

CONCERTO IN G   CONCERTO IN D

Ravel did not attempt to write an important work. A concerto or symphony from the pen of any composer is not without its significance. When it is from a composer of Ravel's standing it assumes a place among its fellows for that reason alone. This was obviously not appreciated when the work was performed for the first time in London, for the critics fell foul of it because of its very virtues of lightness, dexterity and simplicity. Ravel expressly stated that he was not concerned with a concerto against the piano, but with one for it. As has been stated, he intended it as a light work in the nature of a divertimento. That he succeeded cannot be denied. We may not like the music. We may think it is too much a glitter of orchestral and pianistic tinsel, but there is no gainsaying its success as a work of its kind. Apart from the shade of Liszt hovering, very palely, over the cadenza in the first movement, the writing is pure Ravel. There are no finger muddles; the hands do not tend at first sight to get involved in each other. The only difficulty is that the fingers do not have to go on the notes which they expect; but this must not be taken as implying that the pianism does not lie under the hand. On the contrary; it does so lie, but leads in unexpected directions.

The Concerto in D is a different story. Here Ravel attempted to write something important—after all, a concerto of this nature must of necessity carry everything that is unusual with it. The first essential of such a work is that it should not be a 'stunt.' We should not be aware that it is being played with one hand. On the other hand, we have seen in so many places how bad it is for a work for a limited number of instruments to sound as if the players were doing double labour. Is not the avoidance of this the first principle of good quartet writing? Further, the limitations must not be apparent. There must be no place where the deficiency shows up, and nowhere should we feel that if only two hands were available, how very much more could be accomplished. With all these provisos, the composer had considerable responsibility towards his player.

Of course it is largely a matter of visual contact. It cannot be denied that to play a difficult work written for one hand with two is very much easier, and that the provisos mentioned above would seem to preclude any knowledge of the limitations. In radio performances and gramophone recordings who is to know? Perhaps the spreads may be crisper, perhaps the crushing chords sharper than might be possible with one hand —otherwise, what indication can there be? Organists might as well advertise the fact that in some of Bach's organ music they will play a solo with their feet as pianists state that they will play a concerto with one hand. It is all a question of degree. To insist in all cases on the use of one hand is to limit performances, for how many pianists are willing to do with one hand what they can do better with two, and how many have the requisite technique? Ravel's executors may have been wrong when they crabbed Cortot's edition for two hands. There could not have been much alteration in the printed copy, for it is laid out on two staves, and surely no pianist is going to be so mis-guided as to play in public with two hands a work advertised to be played with one. One aspect of the matter is that we do not associate Ravel's music with keys but with descriptions. Hence the announcement of his piano Concerto in G or D leaves the ordinary listener in the dark as to which he is going to hear. That we should be limited to but an occasional performance of the latter because of this difficulty is indeed tragic, for it is splendid music and stirring, a final flash of the Ravel of the *Daphnis et Chloé* days, when he thought broadly and wrote lavishly and richly.

The general spirit of the work is the stateliness of a saraband of large proportions, and Ravel would seem to have finished his career with a final demonstration of his inherent Spanishness. It breathes the atmosphere of a Spanish court richly dressed and ranged in front of opulent tapestries. The courtly grandees of the days of Ferdinand and Isabella prepare to receive their sovereigns and dance a ceremonial saraband—not that the rhythm of this dance is preserved at all in the Concerto. We have seen during the course of this study how Ravel's Spanish temperament per-meated so much of his thought.

Opening with double basses muttering in semiquavers, a rhythmical theme grows out of the orchestra. The double bassoons mark the melody, while the horns dictate the theme shown in Ex. 39. This forms the Introduction to the work, and after a shattering *crescendo* the piano enters with a cadenza, in which the main theme of the movement is announced and worked up. The inclusion of a cadenza at the beginning of a work is unusual, but there is really no reason why a composer should not reverse the usual process and announce his thesis in this manner, for the average cadenza does not contribute very much except restatement of the themes *ad nauseam*. In this particular Concerto we have two cadenzas, so that honour is satisfied all round.

The re-entry of the full orchestra after a 'glissando' on the piano gives us the spirit of a stately *habanera*, although not in any way similar in pace. Ravel seems to have had the knack of suggesting these dance measures or of using their names as a means to his own ends. This is magnificent music, square and precise; we can see the mantillas and cloaks swaying to and fro:

Ex. 40

After storm, the calm. The stress of pageantry is relieved by a fragment which does duty as the second subject. Unfortunately we do not hear it again until the final cadenza:

Ex. 41

From this we pass by way of the opening figure to the scherzo section of the work. This is not particularly full of invention and sounds as if it was very easy to compose. A strongly marked accent gives background and point to consecutive fifths in downward scale and a tune, perky and impertinent, on the piano in single notes, taken up extensively by the bassoon. This is an impudent metamorphosis of the main theme of the work:

Ex. 42

If this reminds us of Dukas and his *L'Apprenti sorcier* it is because of the use of the bassoon in solo, but it is no more reminiscent of that work in material than it is of Gounod's *Funeral March of a Marionette*. Commentators have likened this section to jazz, but it is difficult to see any influence of this whatsoever save in so far as both are highly marked rhythmically.

A dainty passage interrupts the progress of this vivid yet static music, and the bassoon gives us a version of the figure in Ex. 42. Finally there is a superb restatement of part of the opening theme, overwhelming in its majesty and dignity:

Ex. 43

The second cadenza is built largely upon the figure in Ex. 39 and the second subject. It leads straight into the coda founded upon the opening introductory figure, and with a spiteful stamping of the scherzo accent the concerto comes to a sudden end.

There is no doubt that this is one of the best of Ravel's larger works, ranking with *Daphnis et Chloé*. Its pianism is of the virtuoso order, in the old tradition of such things. Nevertheless, it would not do to think that there is anything reactionary in it, although it takes a brave composer nowadays to write an arpeggio on a common chord—and get away with it. Those who feel that Ravel said his last orchestral word in *La Valse* should ponder upon this Concerto.

Thus we have two concertos the direct antithesis of each other. The one, very much *concertante*, light, airy and cheerful; the other, very much a concerto for a solo instrument, dramatic, multi-coloured and even spiteful in the nature of the scherzo. Comparison otherwise is impossible, and it cannot be said that one is any better than the other, for both excel in their several natures and both have certain weaknesses. As to that, one would say that the first movement of the G major flags horribly in the middle and that the dainty passage which relieves the venom of the scherzo in the D major neither convinces by its material and the use of that material, nor justifies itself in the context. But such charges may be levelled at many such works, and they are none the worse for them. Perfection everywhere and every time would be monotonous and unhuman.

Both these works are original and individual in their respective ways. They are unlike any other concertos for any other instruments and thus stand alone and on a sure foundation. Two things militate against frequent performance. The first is the difficulty of finding a trumpet player with sufficient confidence to do himself justice in the first movement of the G major; the second the restriction to performance with the left hand in the case of the D major, a restriction emphasized by the use of its description 'Concerto for the Left Hand.' Rechristen it

'Concerto in D,' let every one forget its original form, and there is no reason why it should not take its place in the regular repertory. In this way it would be available for a greater number of players and would remove any charge of acrobatism from its performance.

Having thus discussed its possibilities from the layman's point of view, we make way for Mr. Clifford Curzon, who has played it several times in this country and completely refutes all our theories from the pianist's angle.[1] Mr. Curzon says that in his opinion the work is so wonderfully written for the left hand that it really would be more difficult to play it with two hands. He says that the reasons are difficult to analyse, but he is inclined to put it down to the fact that

Ravel has given the melodic line to the heavy (thumb) side of the hand where it receives a natural accentuation and singing quality. This is to be noticed especially in the last big cadenza. If, for practice, one picks out the melody notes with the *right* hand, it is surprising how much less well they sound than when they form the natural apex of the left-hand arpeggio figures. The roll of the arpeggio brings the melody note at the right moment musically with the right quality of tone.

He further states in answer to the question 'Is it worth playing with one hand?':

Yes. Not *because* it is written for one hand, but because it is a beautiful piece of music, exquisitely scored (the single hand is always audible) and a splendid addition to the repertory of modern concertos for the piano.

He also feels that

the very limitation from without has stimulated the composer—just as particular voices, etc., inspired other composers from time to time—to a remarkable achievement.

All this goes to show that one must not theorize. It goes also to show that Cortot's action in bringing out an edition for two hands was not only unnecessary but highly ill-advised from the practical point of view.

[1] In a letter to the author dated 19th April 1946.

CHAPTER IX

THE SONGS

RAVEL'S songs divide themselves into three distinct categories, the ordinary *chanson* or *mélodie*—songs with piano accompaniment—settings of *chansons* and *chants populaires* in which the accompaniment alone is Ravel's, and the elaborate 'work' for voice and instruments in which the latter play as important a part as the former. It may be convenient to consider these categories in turn, irrespective of the chronology of each species as a whole.

His first published song, *Sainte* (1896), is notable for its chordal use of sevenths and ninths and a voice-line of extreme simplicity and diatonicism. It is but a trifle, and organists in search of vocal pieces for recitals away from the ordinary run of such things might well give *Sainte* a thought.

The next, *Deux Épigrammes de Clément Marot* (1898), are different. These epigrams concern themselves with a charming person named Anne, *qui me jecta de la neige* and *jouant de l'espinette*. The former commands consideration for its free rhythm. We move, on the first page alone, from 7-4 to 5-4 and 6-4, but this change of time-signature falls naturally and it in no way sounds forced or difficult. The piano part is sad and rather square; like so many youthful efforts, it is too full and thick, but the voice is in no way obscured. Altogether the manner is too heavy for the texture of both poems and melody. In the second he naturally attempts to imitate the spirit of the instrument upon which Anne is playing. The spirit is that of Couperin, but, again, it is not simple enough to balance the slender lyric. Nevertheless, like the first song, this is perfectly charming. These trifles are well worth singing to-day, for they breathe the atmosphere of the French *chanson* and, in addition, reflect their composer's individuality. What was said of the early piano pieces applies equally well to these songs: they bear the stamp of their composer.

We may apply similar sentiments to *Le Noël des jouets* (1905), in which the piano is treated in the style of a guitar.

In 1907 he wrote a *Vocalise en forme d'habanera* which has been transcribed for every imaginable instrument. In its original form it is suggestive of the Spanish strain in his nature and therefore most successful. The term *ravissant* fits it admirably, but that is not to say that there is nothing else to it. Indeed, of all Ravel's Spanish inspirations this one breathes nostalgia and gives us the true essence of its origin.

Nothing else in this category occurs until 1915 when he wrote *Trois Chansons* (to his own words) for mixed chorus, afterwards transcribing them for voice and piano. These three little gems are perfect miniatures: *Nicolette, Trois beaux oiseaux du Paradis* and *Ronde* are of the type which are truly national. They could emanate from no other country than France. The poems are exquisite if naïve, but, alas, the English translation tries our gravity. Even if this translation were approaching adequacy it would be impossible to sing the songs in any language but French to catch their true spirit. It is disconcerting for any singer to be faced with accentuation such as this:

$$\tfrac{2}{4} \text{ and } \breve{e} \smile ve \smile r\bar{y} \smile \mid \text{where}$$

from *Nicolette* and

$$\tfrac{3}{4} \text{ flying dĕv-ils, dĕv-il-kins}$$

from *Ronde*. The strange thing is that, knowing Calvocoressi so well, Ravel did not ask him to translate the poems so that the accents should fall on the right places. In all three songs Ravel simplified himself down to the essentials. The piano punctuates things and leaves the voice untrammelled.

Ronsard à son âme (1924) was Ravel's contribution to the homage paid to Ronsard by *La Revue musicale*. It could not have given him very much trouble. The piano part is mostly in open fifths while the voice delivers the verse *quasi parlando*. It is of no significance whatsoever.

The sum total of this category, therefore, is a number of very charming things, truly French, truly Ravel, which have a place in the canon and should come into the regular repertory of singers as songs representative of the French type of *chanson*.

Of the settings of traditional airs of all races, the most successful is the set of Greek tunes, the words of which were translated by Calvocoressi, himself of Greek origin. Ravel caught the atmosphere of these individual melodies very well and his accompaniments are accompaniments in the true sense. The five songs are orchestrated, the first and fifth, *Le Réveil de la mariée* and *Tout gai!* by Ravel himself, the other three, *Là-bas vers l'église, Quel galant!* and *Chanson des cueilleuses de lentisques* by Manuel Rosenthal. The general atmosphere of the melodies is not far separated from that of the French *chanson*, and Ravel has been particularly happy in the environment. The set appeared in 1907. Two years later he did another which remained unpublished until *La Revue musicale* brought it out as a supplement to the special number in December 1938. It is not successful. Ravel chose the easy paths: the accompaniments consist of repetitions and lack the invention and imagination of the others.

In 1910 there was held at Moscow the fifth 'Concours de la Maison du Lied,' and Ravel contributed seven *Chants populaires,* Spanish, French, Italian, Hebraic, Scottish, Flemish and Russian. Only the first four are published. Of these the fourth is the most interesting for the way in which Ravel avoided obscuring the free rhythm of the air and contented himself with sustaining a single chord over which the efflorescent melody weaves its way. The same principle he applied to the two similar songs written in 1914. The former four examples were orchestrated. It is worthy of repeated mention that it was these three settings, especially the last two, which earned Ravel the opprobium of the anti-Semites—as well as accusations of being anything from Greek to Scottish!

These folksongs must have tickled Ravel's fancy for the unusual. Curious by nature about everything, interested in anything which appeared out of the ordinary, easily diverted from a matter in hand by anything which caught his eye, he found in these accompaniments an opportunity for a certain amount of experiment and restraint. The latter is admirable even though he sometimes uses that easy way.

From these songs we pass on to the elaborate works in which he was able to display his full individuality.

Shéhérazade (1903) has nothing in common with the overture to the unfinished opera which, earlier, had caused such a pother and a fluttering in the academic dovecots. Here we have, on the contrary, music of substance far removed from the *chansons*; a 'work,' in fact, for voice and accompaniment (of an independent and individual nature) for piano, for which it is unsuited, or orchestra for which it was originally written. It will be noticed that much of the mature Ravel orchestral thought transfers quite well to the piano; in these early days the opposite was the case, and those who attempt these songs should beware of the loss of colour and consequent lack of conviction.

The poems are three in number, *Asie, La Flûte enchantée* and *L'Indifférent*. The first is extremely long and distinctly 'atmospheric music':

> Asia! Land of wonderful tales
> Renowned in ancient lore,
> Where fancy's spirit dwells
> Like some fair sleeping empress
> 'Mid her forest in mystery clad.

So runs the rather prosaic translation of Tristan Klingsor's poem. The poem continues to apostrophize the glories and wonders of Asiatic life and people, the voice-part very naturally (in the course of things which evoke pictures) being declamatory and articulated. The interest lies very largely in the picturesque orchestration which prophesies so much of *Daphnis et Chloé*. One could say with considerable justification that Debussy would have treated the words in this manner, one of the few points of contact between these two composers.

In the second number, *The Enchanted Flute*, we have an early instance of Ravel's fondness for accompanying his voice-line with a single instrumental one, a feature found so largely in *L'Enfant et les sortilèges*. The texture here is more slender, and although the voice is again mainly declamatory, it has more bearing upon the instrumental parts.

In the third, *The Indifferent One*, Ravel very nearly writes a real 'song'; but not quite. The accompaniment has little independence and takes its place under the voice-part in a perfectly normal manner. Ravel is dramatic and inviting at the words 'Enter! Perchance a cup will lend thee spirit,' where he simply sustains two instrumental parts, dropping them altogether at the statement of profound regret: 'But no, thou goest.'

These settings of highly imaginative poetry cannot, and should not, be sung with English words. The very essence of the French syllabic articulation is its suppleness off the tongue. 'Comme une musique fausse,' with the sounded final e's, runs off the tongue in a way that 'Like music false in ring' never can, no matter how skilful the singer. Of course, this raises the question of the feasibility of ever singing translations, in which discussion we cannot join here; but it may be hinted that in poems of this nature written in French that language is the only possible one.

It was in the *Histoires naturelles* (1906) that Ravel proclaimed his mastery of the form and raised more scenes of disorder than had ever taken place in his career before its date. These songs were so different from anything before them that perhaps a certain amount of excuse may be granted to the rioters, an excuse which in itself justifies the mastery of the work because it proclaims its vitality. To begin with, audiences were accustomed to *chansons*, that is to say, melodic lines backed up by an accompaniment of thin charm. Not so did the *Histoires naturelles* proceed; here were no tunes with accompaniment. Further, they are humorous, and humour in music is dangerous: to be funny musically is to flirt with the obvious. However, the humour lay not only in the

97

poems themselves, but in Ravel's serio-comic way of handling them. G. Jean-Aubry says:

> The collection of little incisive pieces is well known. . . . Drawn . . . towards this ironic zoology, Maurice Ravel illustrated with a musical commentary five of these biting texts.
>
> He did this with a suppleness of mind and form of which he alone is capable . . . following, it is scarcely necessary to say, each text, word for word, with a musical transcription in which imitative elegance acquires a strangely broadened value; but reproducing the very atmosphere of these brief tales, and creating around these descriptions, which words necessarily restrict in spite of their power of allusion, a broad and floating power of suggestion, at once accurate and minute, of the landscape in which these passages evolve; and installing a musical irony till then unsuspected. . . . Despite whether one liked or disliked this kind of wit, there was in these five songs too much originality and too much skill for them to continue to be disparaged without the risk of ridicule. Apart from a few sectarians who remained fixed on their first attitude, word was then passed round to declare, with an air of dismissing the subject, that it was merely a jest.[1]

These words sum up the situation. Audiences were not then prepared for jesting in music and evidently they were as solemn in those days as they are to-day. However, it was not merely the jesting music or the jesting words which caused offence. It was the novelty of the sound which seemed, no doubt, a series of wrong notes.

Together with the *Trois Poèmes de Mallarmé*, the *Histoires naturelles* are among the most significant works in music, and not only in French music. The set consists of five songs, each of which can truly be credited with saying something that had never been said before; this must be remembered to-day, because much of the idiom is almost stereotyped by now.

1. *Le Paon* (*The Peacock*)

The piano-part is forceful and chordal, typical of the splendour and dignity of the bird in question. The voice-part nears the recitative principle and is sufficiently dramatic at the proper

[1] *French Music of To-day*, translated by Edwin Evans.

moments. If we imagine the audience of that time prepared to listen to a set of *chansons,* this extract will probably suffice to show the severe jolting these preconceived ideas received:

Ex. 44

2. *Le Grillon (The Cricket)*

Here the whole idea is almost imitational. Ravel uses the cricket's chirrup, not in the way that he imitated the birds in *Ma Mère l'Oye,* but far more graphically, with a rhythmic repetition of C♯. Further, this use of close intervals of the second was almost revolutionary: [1]

Ex. 45

The song is even more declamatory than *Le Paon*—the poem describes the usual habits of the cricket minutely and fancifully. It was the silences towards the end which the audience resented and which they filled up with their own noises.

[1] But Haydn's crickets in *The Seasons* already chirp in minor seconds.—ED.

3. *Le Cygne (The Swan)*

Ravel describes a peaceful scene, with the swan floating down-stream. This song has a definite pianism and a clear melodic line, and illustrates the movements of the bird in detailed fashion, especially at the words 'suddenly thrusts his whole neck in the water. Then, as a woman pulls her arm from a sleeve, he draws it back. Nothing there. He looks down, but the fugitive shadows have all vanished.' Of all the five, this one is the most complete and self-contained, and has the most music.

4. *Le Martin-pêcheur (The Kingfisher)*

Sliding sevenths coming to roost on a sustained chord or single note give the atmosphere of a solemn and static bird. The voice-part is entirely declamatory. It was the first line, 'Not a single bite to-day,' which caused such an outburst of jeers on the first performance.

5. *La Pintade (The Guinea-fowl)*

Ravel writes a scintillating *alla scherzando* which gives us a true picture of the guinea-fowl and its cry:

Ex. 46

This passage must have been enough to set the seal on the
indignation of the audience! It is certainly the most descriptive
of the set.

In no place does the voice rely on the instrumental background
and both are of an amazing simplicity. It may perhaps be
wondered how such simplicity could have raised such great
indignation and made the songs so important. The fact is that
Ravel did not set out to do anything but illustrate Jules Renard's
very delicate and not unamusing text. (The excellent English
translation, by the way, is by Nita Cox.) However, it does not
follow that the heavier the music the more important, else are
Strauss, Mahler and Bruckner more important than in actuality.
If a set of songs can change the face of music, it is sufficient that
their texture should be as it is. In contrast, we have but to look
at the earlier *chansons* and *Shéhérazade*. In the latter the canvas
is broad. In the *Histoires naturelles* it is small and in proportion
with that of the *chansons*; the approach to the several texts is
different. Here we have declamation, there melody.

The *Histoires naturelles* show Ravel almost at his top level.
Historically they are of the utmost importance. The fullness of
the conception and the manner in which he maintains independence of thought between the instruments and the voice, thus
heralding the *Trois Poèmes de Mallarmé* (which are considered
advisedly in the chapter on the chamber music), pointed a fresh
directive in the path of vocal music. They may be considered as an exercise in declamation, as Roland-Manuel truly
observes.[1]

Les Grands Vents venus d'outre-mer (1906), to words by Henri
de Régnier, is an ambitious affair in which Ravel contrives a
piano-part independent of the voice—indeed, one is inclined to
see the vocal line as fitted into the instrumental framework. This
is one of the few instances where we find a slight point of contact
with Debussy in its semitonal triadic flow which uses the higher
registers of the piano to give a feeling of repose and poise. The

[1] *A la Gloire de Ravel.*

final cadence might have come from one of the Debussy *Préludes*:

Ex. 47

If *Sur l'herbe* (1907) is not elaborate or ambitious, it comes in this category because, again, the piano-part is too full to be considered a mere accompaniment. The cynicism of Verlaine's poem is admirably caught and the voice-part covers more ground than in *Les Grands Vents*. Ravel indulges his love of major seconds between the extreme notes of the octave. It can be said that the vocal line anticipates to a certain degree the freedom of *Placet futil* in the *Trois Poèmes de Mallarmé*.

There is nothing further in this category until we reach the *Chansons madécasses* (1925-6). These are among the most remarkable works of their kind. Ravel's style had become more abstract, more contrapuntal (as we have seen in the Sonata for violin and cello). He was stimulated by the works of Parny, and the bitterness of human feeling which characterized the *Chansons madécasses* determined the music. The songs, three in number, *Nahandove . . .*, '*Aouo!*' and *Il est doux . . .* were written for flute, cello, piano and voice at the instigation of Mrs. Coolidge. The second created a scene at its first performance in 1925—the complete set was not performed until the following year. War had been declared on Morocco by France and a member of the audience rose up, and after addressing a few remarks to Mme Jane Bathori and to Ravel himself, announced his name and his intention of leaving the hall, not wishing to hear such a song when his country was at war with Morocco. This very proper sentiment seems to have had no more result than did the famous remark of 'Thank God that's over' from a member of the audience at a Philharmonic concert. Both audiences were highly diverted. The Frenchman did at least give his name.

The song in question is probably the most bitter and spiteful outcry that one can think of. 'Aoua! Méfiez-vous des blancs habitants du rivage.' The scream of rage with which it opens is a far cry from the tenderness of the earlier *chansons* and the *Introduction and Allegro*. Ravel was incapable of writing quasi-orientalism, and we may take it that there was authority in his mind for the idiom of this song, which uses the flute in its low register on a melodic line centralized on D$\sharp$, the line itself being strictly limited in scope, over a punctuating piano-part of hard sevenths. In this music we hear a summary of the whole question of race hatred.

In the first, *Nahandove,* Ravel again uses the piano as a per-cussive, punctuating instrument, the cello playing an individual line, while the voice declaims the verse.

The third, *Il est doux . . . ,* almost defies analysis. The piano sustains a low open fifth while the voice weaves a melodic line of great passion, albeit a tender passion, which is accentuated by its limited range.

Not only are the *Chansons madécasses* unique in the Ravel canon, but we can think of no other songs which form a parallel. Their effect is gained by economy of means, and although the flute is directed to sound like a trombone, this direction does not attempt to alter the natural scope of the instrument.

The last work in this *genre* was a *chanson* to words by Fargue, *Rêves,* in which Ravel uses another limited melody over an accom-paniment of rhythmic similarity, giving the song an atmosphere of gentle rest and quietness.

What Shaliapin would have made of the songs for the *Don Quixote* film is not difficult to guess. An operatic star of enor-mous power and self-determination, always tending to bend the music to his own will, he would have been flabbergasted at this music which in no place seeks to demonstrate the singer's vocal prowess. Based on Basque and Spanish themes and laid out with extreme literalness, tenderness and simplicity, it would have been completely overpowered by the great Russian singer. The film company no doubt thought of this when they decided on another composer; they might have done so from the first; but then we should not have had these last exquisite examples of the gentle Ravel, and that would have been an incalculable loss.

Ravel used the Spanish idiom of which he was such a natural master. In the first, *Chanson romantique*, he alternates a 6–8 and a 3–4 rhythm over an accompaniment of a guitar nature. The same process is employed in the second, *Chanson épique*. The third, *Chanson à boire*, is in the spirit of the *jota* with its characteristic strong rhythms and vigour. Here the spirit is ironical and the orchestration extremely subtle. Ravel sang himself into silence in his own inimitable fashion.

CHAPTER X

'DAPHNIS ET CHLOÉ'—'LA VALSE'—'BOLERO'

Daphnis et Chloé supplies the answer to those who question Ravel's ability to write extended works. That he was not in the habit of doing so was probably due to his not wanting to—indeed, in his article on Ravel in Grove's Dictionary M. D. Calvocoressi goes so far as to state categorically that the characteristic was 'due to a deliberate carefully thought-out aesthetic choice.' *Gaspard de la nuit* is another case in point.

Ravel described *Daphnis et Chloé* as a 'Choreographic Symphony in three parts.' Symphony in the usually applied and accepted form it certainly is not. At the same time it is not written in 'ballet form,' that is, split up into 'Pas seul,' 'Pas d'action,' 'Adagio,' 'Variation,' 'Coda,' etc. He maintained that it is 'constructed symphonically on a very strict tonal plan, with a number of themes whose developments assure the homogeneity of the work.' [1]

However, it would be impossible to analyse it in the usual manner. It might appear from this that it is hermaphroditic or amorphous, neither the one thing nor the other. One thing it certainly is—remarkably beautiful music.

During the latter part of my military career I was much occupied with 'music in the forces' (there being little else for either myself or the forces to do) in A.-A. Command. One of the games we used to play was 'guessing the meaning.' This meant that a record of descriptive music was played on the gramophone and every one wrote down what he or she thought it was all about. One of the standard examples was 'Dawn of Day' from *Daphnis et Chloé*, and the majority invariably guessed right—and none of

[1] Biographical sketch.

them had ever seen the work or even heard it. If successful music for ballet is that which is indivisible from the stage in that it underlies everything indisputably, *Daphnis et Chloé* would appear to be perfect for its purpose; but music for ballet is very often unsatisfactory by itself because its various movements are terse and lacking both personality and development.

Daphnis et Chloé is successful both in the theatre and in the concert-hall; yet it is neither bad theatre nor bad concert music. It is apt for the theatre because of its rhythms. It is apt for the concert-hall because of its themes and its orchestration—its colour.

Ravel tells us that he was 'anxious less about archaicism than fidelity to the Greece of my dreams, which is that which the French artists at the end of the eighteenth century imagined and painted.' [1] Apart from a few bars of quasi-modal writing, therefore, the idiom is sheer French romanticism, and for this we may be thankful.

Ravel employs an enormous orchestra, complete with wind machine and a mixed-voice chorus, vocalizing. (In 1907 he wrote a *Habanera* for vocalization with piano accompaniment.) This colossal requirement has, of course, militated against performance in its original form as a ballet. The chorus is doubled in the orchestra with one notable exception when it sings entirely *a cappella*. To the suggestion that in this 'land of the choral tradition' such an extra as a choir should be no difficulty, the answer is that Ravel does not write in the English choral tradition, and our choral societies would be hard put to it to master the complexities of attack and intonation, to say nothing of the fact that they are not necessarily operatically trained. However, a concert performance would be possible—but that is, after all, only a makeshift for a genuine performance in the original form.

It is a spectacular work in so far as the producer has many opportunities and the scenic designer equal scope. The scene is a grotto in a sacred wood. On a rock are the figures of three

[1] Biographical Sketch.

nymphs, sculptured in an archaic style. On the left there is a large rock not unlike the figure of Pan, half-man, half-goat. Sheep are grazing. It is a clear, sunny afternoon.

The music is vague and nebulous. Over a pedal A it rises in sustained perfect fifths up to the high D♯. Tonally it hovers round E and A, but finally resolves on to a first inversion of the dominant ninth in B♭, a typical Ravel change which other French composers have indulged in (Vincent d'Indy has a some-what similar modulation in the prelude to *Fervaal*). It is a characteristic of *Daphnis et Chloé*.

At once we have the first of the themes which are the bases of the whole work and which should be noted. They appear frequently and are easily recognizable, for there is little if any development of them and their changes do not disguise them in any way.

Ex 48

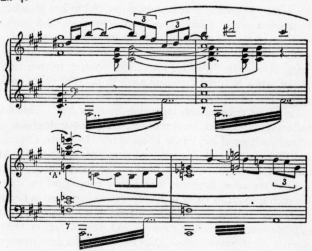

The theme marked 'A' is the most important in the whole

work. The other is a flute figure which later becomes thematically important:

Ex. 49

Young men and girls bring in gifts of fruit for the Nymphs. The music becomes more definite—triplets of quavers with a three-note rhythm underneath, repeated at different pitches for some while. The actual mime of bringing in and laying down the votive offerings being over, the worshippers break into a *Danse religieuse* of smooth line, which flows in a dignified manner, always over a firm bass. The chorus is vocalizing throughout on the figure of Ex. 48 in the middle register. It presses on, never reaching a very high dynamic, until Daphnis enters, leading his flock. Immediately we hear the theme 'A' in Ex. 48, which is repeated when Chloe joins him. Here we find further evidence of Ravel's obsession with the interval of the second.

The religious dance is renewed and increases to an intensity, dying down when Daphnis and Chloe re-enter, to their tune, played over a sustained dominant ninth in E. The dance stops, and to Ex. 49 there is 'sweet emotion at the sight of the couple.'

Let us get certain points quite clear from the start. This is a ballet about innocence, innocence surprising among shepherds to whom the 'facts of life' should be no secret. However, Daphnis and Chloe are indeed innocent, and seem perfectly content to let their love be consummated in kisses. One would imagine that some of the other shepherds would have enlightened the pair; but such is youth, or rather such it appears to have been in Greek mythology. Hence, the other inhabitants of the island view this calf-love with sentimental pleasure, and do not care to break down a pretty picture. Both Daphnis and Chloe are extremely popular with their fellows. One must admit that Ravel has caught this spirit very well in his choice of theme.

The young girls draw Daphnis into their dance. This is a brittle affair in 7-4 time, lively, rhythmic and calculated to make the dancers think and count hard so as not to get tied up with that extra beat. Its clear-cut rhythm continues with unabated tightness. Chloe resents the girls' attentions to Daphnis, but she is, in turn, seized by the young men and made to dance with them, which she does tantalizingly and in all innocence. A young shepherd named Dorcon has other views besides those of dancing. He is a young drunkard, and Ravel makes his music assume a smooth and smeary colour.

A *Danse générale* follows, at the end of which there is some miming in which the music, apart from one passage, is necessarily perfunctory. The passage in question we might designate 'The Kiss,' and it should be noted because later it appears with its full force and significance:

Ex. 50

Dorcon tries to embrace Chloe who, innocently enough, is perfectly willing. Daphnis strikes the young drunkard and goes tenderly and reproachfully to Chloe. He is prevented from reaching her by the young men, who decide that Dorcon and Daphnis shall dance in turn, and the better dancer shall be rewarded by a kiss from Chloe.

Dorcon dances grotesquely—to music as empty as any composer could possibly write. Strident, violent, yes; but musically devoid of any ideas. This kind of thing is very easy to bring off on the orchestra, and as long as it is rhythmic it is bound to be effective.

The crowd laughs ironically at Dorcon's absurd gestures

with an orchestral laugh as graphic as Kodály's sneeze in
Háry János.

'The Kiss' shows us that Daphnis's turn has come. With the
thought of the prize he dances to music happy and tender. This
little piece is almost the only movement which can be played as
a piano solo. In it we see the characteristic simplicity of the
common chord and later we find the following pianism which
reminds us of the earlier *Noctuelles* in shape, if not in substance:

Ex. 51

This is so thoroughly pianistic that transferred to the orchestra
it needs enormous skill in the practice and an equal amount of
imagination in the thinking of it.

Daphnis is awarded the prize—the issue was never really in
doubt! Dorcon tries to claim it as well; he is chased away by
the laughing crowd who are struck dumb suddenly by the sight
of the innocent embrace—to an ineffably lovely scoring of Ex. 48 'A'.
The crowd retires, taking Chloe with them. This kind of love
is incredible. Daphnis is left alone, stupefied with the experience
of the kiss, innocent, feeling that there should be something to

follow but not knowing (and being unable to define) exactly what. He lies flat on the ground, resting his chin on his hands.

To a cynical passage in thirds, Lyceion enters. She is a married woman with lustful designs on Daphnis. She sees him lying there and, coming up behind him, covers his eyes with her hands. He thinks it is Chloe, but is disappointed. Lyceion dances tantalizingly. As if by chance she drops one of her veils. (Fokin used this symbolic gesture in his ballet version of *L'Après-midi d'un faune*.) Daphnis covers his shoulders with it. Ironically she continues her dance, which becomes increasingly langorous; another veil is dropped. Daphnis picks it up, but in spite of the mocking Lyceion, he is strangely disturbed. In the original story by Longus at this point Lyceion proceeds to show Daphnis exactly what she is after, but in the ballet all becomes bustle and confusion. Suddenly there is a clash of arms and loud war-cries are heard. Some women rush in, pursued by a horde of pirates.

Daphnis is terror-stricken lest Chloe may be in danger—he is warned of this by a trumpet theme; he rushes off to help her. Chloe herself appears from the opposite direction and hides behind a tree, in the greatest terror. She throws herself before the altar of the Nymphs. The orchestra thunders out a broad rhythmic figure and the pirates seize Chloe and carry her off.

Daphnis reappears—this game of hide-and-seek slightly strains our gravity. He sees a sandal on the ground. He recognizes it as belonging to Chloe. In despair he curses the gods who have not protected her and falls senseless at the entrance to the grotto. As in all the other mimed episodes, the music is perfunctory; it dies down to a *pianissimo*.

A glimmering light fills the passage. To the theme of Ex. 49 a little flame appears suddenly on the heads of the statues. The statues (Nymphs) leave their pedestals and dance slowly and mysteriously.

They lead Daphnis towards the grotto and invoke the aid of Pan. The figure of the god grows clearer as Daphnis supplicates him. From a distance we hear voices singing, and the effect, after a long stretch of orchestral sound, is wonderful. Ravel here adopts a quasi-ecclesiastical style in his two-bar peroration:

Ex. 52

The rocking figure continues for some time, and it is not till the fourth page of this lovely writing that any instrument is heard. We may compare this writing for mixed voices with our own 'English tradition.' The French composer is not concerned with the difficulties of attack; thus against a tenor B♯ the second sopranos come in on C♯, an octave higher, with no preparation. Harmonically the Frenchman is more sensuous than an Englishman would be. The sopranos move in major seconds, and steady intonation is needed for the upward semitonal scales. Ravel expects much from his singers, although the individual lines are reasonably easy; he has in mind the use of the voices as an added orchestral timbre.

A distant trumpet-call signifies further approaching danger.

The scene changes. A camp of pirates is discovered on the seashore and a trireme is drawn up on the sands. The pirates are running hither and thither with their arms full of loot. The *Danse guerrière* which follows is violent and brutal. Rhythmically it is regular—one calls to mind a similar dance in Roussel's *Aeneas*, another ballet demanding a chorus. The direction is *animé et très rude*. A rhythmic figure acts as a kind of ground, appearing at the top as well as at the bottom. The rhythm is changed to one of six quavers from one of four, and eventually the tenors and basses join in. The volume increases, and with a crash the dance suddenly stops.

What was said about Dorcon's grotesque dance applies equally here. There is no invention—and no music. Borodin and Stravinsky did this kind of thing much better. Still, as a means of whipping up brutal excitement, it is effective; but it is not quite exciting enough and, as music, it is dull.

The pirates send for Chloe and order her to dance. Reluctantly she does so, to music graceful and plaintive. Ravel directs that every other bar shall be played *rallentando* and a curiously tired and pathetic effect results. Twice Chloe tries to escape, but each time she is held back. She thinks of Daphnis (Ex. 48 'A'). Stung to impatience, the leader of the pirate gang (we advisedly refrain from calling him the Pirate King!) lifts her up in triumph; but suddenly the atmosphere becomes charged with something sinister. Little lights flicker and fantastic figures leap hither and thither. The pirates are terrified. Satyrs spring up from all directions and surround the gang. The earth trembles and Pan's profile is seen outlined against the mountains in a menacing attitude. The pirates fly for their lives.

The stage is deserted, and Chloe stands motionless, a luminous crown appearing on her head. To soft bass semitonal passages the scene changes to that of the opening tableau. It is night. Daphnis is before the entrance to the grotto. The murmur of streams and waterfalls is heard. As day breaks the birds wake up. A shepherd crosses the stage, playing his pipe. The sun struggles to pierce the morning haze. The voices are heard singing their original figure. Herdsmen look for Daphnis and Chloe. They find Daphnis and wake him up. He looks round for Chloe. He sees her and they throw themselves into each other's arms. Daphnis sees the crown of flame on Chloe's head. He knows it to be a manifestation of Pan's intervention.

The music paints a wonderful picture. Under a rustling figure on flutes the bass instruments grope their way in a semitonal passage that puts us into the darkness through which the sun is trying to penetrate. A four-note theme is heard over a low D pedal-point, which rises higher and higher until its climax is reached, when, on an ordinary chord of B minor, we can almost feel the warmth of the first sun-rays. Ravel here supplies the answer to the charge of being unable to draw an extended melodic line, and it is well worth quoting at length. Its ancestry lies in the *Petit Poucet* tune in *Ma Mère l'Oye*. Note its simplicity, its diatonicism:

Ex. 53

Eventually the sun breaks through and day dawns in all its splendour. From here for some time the stage business is mimed, but unlike other places where the music is the background none of it is perfunctory.

The old shepherd Lammon explains to the lovers that if Pan has saved Chloe, it is in memory of the nymph Syrinx, with whom he was once smitten. For some unknown reason Daphnis and Chloe proceed to mime the episode, which seems a waste of time, after all they have been through. Daphnis cuts a stalk and pretends to play on it, as upon a flute. Chloe dances. This music is thoroughly *ravissant*. French composers have a happy knack of writing for the flute both in solo and in *ensemble*, and French flautists a similar skill in making it sound plaintive and melancholy.

Chloe dances to a rapid figure full of light and sparkle. Daphnis grows more disturbed. At length he is driven frantic. Chloe throws herself into his arms. They make their vows before the altar of the nymphs, with an offering of two sheep. This brings Ex. 48 and Ex. 50 together for the last time, a supreme musical moment:

Ex. 54

The rite has been completed. A crowd of young girls, dressed as Bacchantes, with tambourines, fills the stage, followed by a crowd of young men, and a joyous tumult follows.

Ravel may not have had his heart in the grotesque or war dances, but he certainly put it into the final *Danse générale*. This is among the most exciting music ever written. I well remember finding myself standing on the seat with a number of otherwise ordinary Britishers, clapping and shouting like a native at a performance in Paris in 1937. The actual thematic material is slight and one theme open to question. This bears a startling resemblance to Rimsky-Korsakov's *Sheherazade*, but an examination shows that it is only the opening interval and rhythm. The resemblance is apparent and not real.

The main theme is repeated over and over again. Otherwise the music consists of rushing semitonal triplets with a well-marked bass. (The piano score is completely inadequate in every way.) Daphnis and Chloe join in. Soon Dorcon takes part, forgiven for his presumption. We shall consider the orchestration in another chapter, suffice it to say that the trumpets have a field-day with their sliding triads.

The piano score omits one tremendous moment when Ex. 48 'A' is thundered out in one of the most overwhelming climaxes in music. The riot gets out of hand, and with a great chordal trill the work ends on an ordinary chord of A minor.

Even those who are not of the 'Ravel following' admit that *Daphnis et Chloé* is one of the landmarks in French music. Its position as a ballet is as high as that of *Petrushka*. Although it does not say as much as *The Rite of Spring* in the way of astonishing sounds, it reveals many beauties in the matter of orchestration which were new; and its influence is still felt. It forms in itself a text-book on the subject of the orchestra.

Exactly what constitutes great music has never been decided, unless it is its effect on posterity. It is too early to apply this test to *Daphnis et Chloé*. It may not be great music, but it is a great work; ballet is not a medium for music which can ever be a candidate for greatness unless the whole thing, in all its component parts, contributes something importantly fresh. Such is the case with *Petrushka* and *The Rite*. Extravagant claims have been made for both these works—certainly they both said something new, but while the former has undoubtedly had an influence on music, the latter has been a dead end, because it exhausts the resources of the entire gamut of harmony, melody and orchestration. The music of neither work is 'great,' unless weight of tone and complicated rhythms make it so. In no ballet is there time for anything approaching development of material, and the essence of the quality lies in its snappiness and terseness. A length of line such as we find in 'Dawn of Day' is quite exceptional—and this particular movement is certainly not 'danceable.' It is essentially music which underlines scenic display; it is remarkable that the part of *Daphnis et Chloé* which is of the highest standard is this movement which is not danced. It is graphic enough to explain itself. When we listen to it in the concert-hall we can forget its original purpose and hear it as a piece of descriptive music, revelling in its sweep of line, its fullness of scoring, its passionate harmonies.

Let us face the fact that it is no more a symphony than is *Petrushka*, and no more a ballet than is Berlioz's *Symphonie fantastique*. The term 'symphony' is used in a loose manner in France. Here we mean—what we mean. There it often includes the literal meaning of the word 'sound.' Although Ravel himself talked about the development of themes, there is very little of this. Repetition, yes; variation, yes; but symphonic development, no. As for the tonal plan, the tonality is usually obvious, but there is little evidence of tonal relationships.

The story itself is truncated. Fokin merely took the facts and episodes as he wanted them. Thus we can say that it concerns two young lovers; the girl is carried off by pirates; she is rescued by satyrs; she is united with her lover. That is all. Why, then, is Lyceion introduced at all? In the original story she is a married woman with a passion for Daphnis and shows him 'the facts of life,' so that he can consummate his love for Chloe—at the same time being able 'to ease her own desire.' [1] Further than her one brief appearance, we see her not, and at the *dénouement* the orchestra tells us that, in the ballet at least, Daphnis had no need of instruction! Perhaps the enacting of the Pan and Syrinx episode played some part in the lovers' enlightenment. The whole story is one of frustration, and we are not altogether clear when watching the ballet if or when that frustration ends. However, we would not be without that lovely dance of Chloe.

Daphnis et Chloé would make a marvellous film—and this is not to speak in any derogatory manner. The miming is always intelligible, and there is such fine music.

It is sometimes disillusioning to inquire too deeply into our favourite music; but we give the following for what it is worth. In an article *Maurice Ravel and the Basque Country* [2] Gustave Samazeuilh writes:

[1] George Moore, *Pastoral Loves of Daphnis and Chloe* (Heinemann).
[2] *La Revue musicale*, December 1938.

. . . I heard him one day . . . strumming out a theme which resembled like a twin brother, both in melodic shape and harmoniza-tion, one of those from a piece I had composed for the piano, *Naïades au soir*, which Alfred Cortot played the preceding year at the Société Nationale, orchestrated later, but which Ravel had not then heard. It had become the theme of the Nymphs in *Daphnis et Chloé* and fitted so well that I immediately insisted that Ravel—who at first would not listen to me, and was not of a mind to find anything else—should change nothing owing to this purely fortuitous coincidence, and, so far as I was concerned, of no importance. . . . The day that the score of *Daphnis* was published, I received a presentation copy with an affectionate note: 'To the composer of the principal theme of this work.'

Such musical coincidences are easy to find. It is not the use of the theme which matters, but the way it is used.

Daphnis et Chloé will live, if only in the two sets of 'Symphonic Fragments' which appear in our concert programmes with en-couraging frequency. As a complete work it takes its place amongst the greatest for the theatre, and certainly one of the greatest ever composed by a Frenchman.

La Valse, it will be remembered, started life as a kind of sym-phonic poem glorifying Vienna and entitled *Wien*. Later it was renamed and danced by Ida Rubinstein.

It attempts no more than to provide a stage spectacle, although in the concert-hall it appears a perfectly normal introduction and *valse viennoise*. If we refer back to the chapter in which Ravel explains his intention in the work, we shall see that it opens with a vague cloudy scene in which couples are waltzing. This misty effect is admirably pictured in the music with low bass and cello tremolos. We hear a fragment of the main theme rising up through the haze. The haze clears away, not *fortissimo* as many other composers would have let it do, but still *pianissimo*, while a theme in thirds slowly threads it passage over an irregularly grouped row of quavers. Eventually the climax is reached. The work introduces several themes until, with an almost drunken stagger, the whole orchestra thunders out its swirling melodies. In the middle we get a short return of the opening misty passage which, if we apply the argument too closely, becomes illogical; but it is not possible or feasible to carry on this coloured orgy without some break in the movement. The dance pushes on to its riotous coda.

Although there are some good melodic lines, it is the orchestral colour which makes the work. It is a veritable *tour de force* which some think the height of vulgarity and others the acme of orchestral resource. All depends on the point of view. Ravel enjoys himself on the orchestra and lets his fancies run riot as they please. If the approach is from a symphony by Sibelius, then the whole of *La Valse* sounds tawdry and tinselly. Take the work as it was intended and we find it a perfectly balanced type of *valse viennoise* on a big scale, an apotheosis of a gay city in its heyday. The trouble with it in the theatre is its brevity, although that brevity should commend it physically to dancers. However, a well-known ballet conductor, Antal Dorati (of Colonel de Basil's Ballet Russes), told me that a work lasting less than thirty minutes was not worth while (he evidently forgot Balakirev's *Tamara*).

Ravel indulges in an enormous orchestra of which the percussion section is unusually complete; it will suffice to say that the scoring is the work of a virtuoso composer for the orchestra. Ravel intended it to be opulent and rich in colour. He succeeded in his intention. It is indeed magnificent in sound and within its limits echoes the old Viennese waltzes of Schubert in spirit, if it exceeds them in size and verve. It makes the *Valses nobles et sentimentales* seem very small.

About the *Bolero* a great deal of nonsense has been spoken and written. Extravagant claims have been made for it—the Ravel tributes in France place far too much emphasis on it—and an equal amount of silly derogation has shown the detractors to be devoid of humour and ignorant of the facts. After its first performance in London it was suggested that since it was a *crescendo* for orchestra, someone should write a *decrescendo* and perform both works together. Some saw in it the final loss of musicality which they had been watching in its approach for some years.

It is absurd to perform it in a concert-hall unless there is a full synopsis in the programme; but then, that is the case of *Petrushka*. We have seen how the *Bolero* came into being and Ravel's attitude towards it. The whole scenic basis justifies the music, whether the music was composed first and the scenario added afterwards or the other way round.

The café is empty except for some chairs and tables, and a dancer. She dances alone. The stage gradually fills up and the tables are occupied. Still the dancer dances alone. Someone feels himself impelled to join her. He does so, and the onlookers add themselves pair by pair until the whole stage is a swirling mass of bodies. Hence the orchestral *crescendo*: its logic is so sure that it is difficult to think of the work in any other way.

Its effect in the concert-hall was duly noted by the writer at its first concert performance in Paris. The monotony, far from being soporific, was almost aphrodisiacal. Its insistence played upon the senses to an inordinate degree. People clutched each other and crumpled their programmes into lumps of perspiring pulp. The effect increased until that terrific change to E major, when the effect was that of a pricked bubble. One could hear the gasp as the tension was released.

Of course, this does not happen a second time. Mesmeric forces of this kind can work on the ear only once. Thereafter it becomes a joke and even that palls after a few minutes. The worst of musical jokes is that they must die after one telling— would that this were so everywhere! For this reason the work might be allowed to drop out of the concert repertory altogether. It is interesting to remember the host of small combinations which played it in a truncated form.

Ravel does not stint himself in instruments. One oboe player doubles the oboe d'amore. There are a clarinet in E♭ and a bass clarinet, trumpet in D and three saxophones as addenda to the ordinary orchestral lay-out. His love of pedal-points is emphasized by the insistent rhythm which continues relentlessly on the side drum:

The theme itself is divided into three parts, and by the time the *tutti* has been reached each of the treble instruments has played at least one section. The tune is insidious and compelling because of the repetition. It is quite gay, especially the first part.

Ex. 55

Finally it is spread out in common chords (root position) on the violins (four parts) doubled by trumpets, trombones and saxophones. The rest of the orchestra plays like a gigantic guitar, with the percussion rattling out the pedal rhythm. For sixty-two pages of the miniature score (and a certain number of pages are divided into two) the tonic and dominant—C and G—are thrashed out with square energy, until the middle of page 63 when the music makes that startling transition to the key of E— but only for eight bars, after which it returns to C for its coda, trombones indulging in some rude-sounding slides. It ends with a plagal cadence.

It is a bolero only in name. This was used simply as the title to the ballet. It is too slow in pace and the rhythm is all wrong. A bolero is exceedingly gay and dashing. Its importance rests on its originality. It signifies nothing either musically or physically, if we refer that term to the composer's alleged decay of musicality. In another sense it does signify a physical state which is relieved and released at the change of key. One feels at that moment that if he had gone on for another bar he 'would have had to marry the girl.' Conductors do not like it very much.

CHAPTER XI

CHAMBER MUSIC

THE string Quartet, written in 1902–3, was revised and published by Ravel in 1910. To what extent the revised version differs from the original we do not know, and it does not matter. It may be regarded as an act of faith on the part of the composer that he had sufficient confidence in his comparatively early works to issue them when he had reached maturity. The *Habanera* is another case in point.

The Quartet is an important work, as important as Debussy's one Quartet. A comparison between these works is not necessary; both contributed new lines of thought and approach to the quartet species. Ravel took the line that the four string instruments called for sweetness rather than vigour (although the scherzo has this element) and for no violence. The usual manner of considering a string quartet is to regard it as a work for four soloists of equally high attainments playing their own individual lines which, combined, give the work contrapuntal facility and expression. The Quartet has always been regarded as a particularly pure medium and one in which there must be no tricks or effects simply for their own sake. In this way it differs from the mode of writing for string orchestra. The essence is counterpoint, not harmony.

Ravel shed a new light on these theories and proved that it was possible for a composer to place counterpoint second, the first essential being the making of lovely sounds without any suggestion of programmatic or even romantic background. In this respect his string Quartet is a landmark in the history of chamber music and a beacon in the history of French music.

The reader of the score and the listener to the music will find very few devices such as adorn the works of the older classical composers, although there are several points which show Ravel to have been not incapable of indulging in them in a mild way. Had he written a second Quartet after the Sonata for violin and cello, when his outlook had become more severe and erudite, it is probable that he would have conformed very largely to the established ideas and ideals. As it was, he remained content to forge his own way ahead, and this led in the opposite direction. If a composer is to be known by his powers of development, his ability to make things grow out of nothing, his skill in expansion, then Ravel was of no great moment and Bruckner the greatest composer who ever lived. These attributes, however, are not the signs by which we recognize a great composer, although we acknowledge them and bow to the intellect which gave them birth. Ravel was never a manufacturer, a carpenter who could cut and turn his materials into all kinds of imaginable shapes, although it must be admitted that he had this ability; otherwise his studentship at the Conservatoire with Gédalge and Fauré would have led to naught and been in vain. It was that this particular means of approach to music did not appeal to him, that he did not want to conform to the established ideas of development. It would never do to assume that he was incapable of them, as so many presume to do. His particular genius led him to the aesthetic more than to the intellectual aspects of musical creation, and we can see in the later Sonata for violin and cello that, had he wished, he could have turned out contrapuntal works with the best of them.

The string Quartet, therefore, is important since it strikes out along paths of sheer expressionism, and that without any pictorial basis—it is notable that only in the chamber music (and the piano Sonatina) does Ravel eschew this pictorial background until the last two big works, the two piano Concertos, are reached. The music moves gracefully and easily. Dedicated to Gabriel Fauré and written under his influence (as any work must be when composed by a musician revering his master as Ravel revered

Fauré) it has all the charm of Fauré plus a colour and a leaning to certain resources which were absent from Fauré's chamber music. Fauré might have written parts of the first movement; he probably would not have written the scherzo; he would have aimed at more continuity in the slow movement; while the finale is as far outside the Fauré canon as anything could be expected. Not knowing exactly how the work stood before its revision, we cannot tell just what Fauré 'passed' and what Ravel discarded and rewrote. Assuming that the revision did not entail a re-writing of the essentials, we should be glad that Fauré had vision to give his pupil his head and did not try to superimpose his own ideas, as so many teachers are prone to do.

The work is in four movements. The first opens with a graceful rising passage of which use is made constantly throughout the work:

Ex. 56

The rising tenths in the violin and cello give the music elevation. Formally, it is in ternary form, quite distinctly. The connecting episode introduces a new tune over a perfunctory inner part, the whole being set firmly on a pedal:

Ex. 57

The second subject, led into by a repeated dominant A, affords
us an early glimpse of a typically Ravellian characteristic, a
characteristic which was to remain with him all his life, that of
doubling the tune at the fifteenth. This subject, as diatonic as
could be wished (like the principal subject), presages those long
similar tunes in *Ma Mère l'Oye* and *Daphnis*:

Ex. 58

Underneath are no contrapuntal devices, simply a *tremolo* on
the second violin punctuated by a *pizzicato* bass. The figure
marked 'A' becomes significant because it is used as a link
between the second subject and the middle section (the codetta
of the classical sonata) and introduces it later as a kind of binding
figure.

Under a violin *tremolo* the viola refers to the second subject, the principal subject appearing thinly disguised at different times. The recapitulation is led into by an augmentation of the first three notes of the principal subject. The coda is based on Ex. 58 'A,' and the movement closes with a combination of two fragments of the first and second subjects.

The ear must be prepared for repetition. Ravel pursues a little section of a theme relentlessly, and this repetitiveness, far from being a vice, becomes a virtue because it is part of the Ravel technique.

In the scherzo we get cross-rhythms. A two-bar phrase in triple time over a strongly marked compound duple figure is hammered at indefatigably, to be relieved by a suave three-bar phrase extended to four by repetition of the first bar:

Ex. 59

Ex. 60

These are combined with no little ingenuity and the whole section is repeated. The first trio, marked *Lent*, reminds us of Ex. 60 over a new tune on the cello:

Ex. 61

Considerable repetition of Ex. 60 follows and a piquant variation of the first bar of Ex. 59 thrown from cello to viola, from
violin to violin:

Ex. 62

leads straight into a full-blooded combination of a variant of the
cello tune in Ex. 61 with the opening figure of the movement. The
solid pedal F gives a satisfactory feeling of strength while the viola
arpeggios fill in the necessary harmonies, giving the section a kind
of synthetic movement, quite contrary to the established canons
of quartet writing.

References to the opening figure, this time in E minor and G♯
minor, bring us back to the scherzo, which return is fundamentally
the same as at the opening, with a scintillating and powerful coda.

The slow movement is a curiously formless rhapsody introducing
familiar material from time to time. It is exceedingly difficult to
apply any yard-stick of formal design to it, for the general idea
appears scrappy and disconnected. In this way we may regard
it as yet another sign of the breaking away from tradition which
Ravel, consciously and subconsciously, persistently strove at, and
it is useless to conclude from this very disjointedness that he was
incapable of anything else. This aspect has been perhaps unduly
accentuated in these pages, but there has always been a tendency

to suppose that incompetence and inability lay at the bottom of his abstinence from classical development. This is clearly wrong because, after all, the Conservatoire was an institution with iron discipline and method for its students.

This free rhapsody design, with only an occasional break into continuity, is not without its fascination for the listener. It relieves him from following the course of the melodic lines, and the aural faculties are exercised only in bathing in the freedom of expression, finding them puzzling at times as to the exact symbolism of a section and its relation to its successors. The movement seems like a conversation between four people at cross-purposes. Every now and again we get a reference to the little tune from the connecting episode of the first movement, so like the principal subject, yet so different. This reference to previous material serves to hold the Quartet together as a whole, but it does not become obvious in this work until the finale, when the quoted material is an integral subject of the movement.

This slow movement defying analysis, we can but draw attention to its constituent parts as they occur. It opens with a little rhythmic figure appearing from time to time during the course of the music, under which another figure—one can hardly call it a tune or a theme—is displayed prominently at different periods:

Ex. 63

A fluttering figure between the two violins in contrary motion brings us to a variant of 'A.' A definite theme appears in the viola for five bars and is succeeded by the first reference to the first movement:

Ex. 64

More placid writing, and the variant comes in once more. Another clear-cut theme appears in the viola:

Ex. 65

This carries on for a short while until the flow is interrupted by a hard re-entry of the rhythmic figure in Ex. 63. After still further discussion of this figure, a long-drawn-out theme begins on the second violin with arpeggio passages above it, and combined at its third bar with Ex. 64:

Ex. 66

The theme delineated in Ex. 66 reappears complete, and the movement ends with further consideration of preceding material.

It may seem from this that the movement is unsatisfactory to listen to; this is not the case. In spite of its disjointedness it is pleasant to consider it in the light of a discussion between four people. That it gets nowhere and amounts to very little is quite in keeping with its cadenza-like spirit. One will never hum it or remember it in the way one remembers and hums the slow movement of the Debussy Quartet; but this is beside the point because the message is different. Debussy deals with clearly pointed melodies; Ravel is concerned entirely with discursive and conversational matters.

The last movement is a *tour de force* of vigour and pleasantry. The opening bar may be regarded as an inverted ground, for it is repeated over and over again with emphatic chords in the first place, succeeded by parallel reiterations. This reiteration is considered as a purely orchestral effect:

Ex. 67

The remainder of the movement consists of reminiscences of the first movement. Both subjects recur and the music has tremendous drive. The work ends with a relentless repetition of the figure opening the movement.

This Quartet stands alone. It is so individual and characteristic of Ravel that any attempt to write one along its own lines must end in either plagiarism or pastiche—the latter because it is not now a modern work, but one representative of a period. The same applies to the Debussy work. Both are fatally easy to copy unconsciously. The Ravel Quartet gives us music polished and pure, as delightful to play as to listen to. Of the four movements, one would say that the first shows most continuity, in spite of the repetition. The second is distinctly original in matter as is the third in manner, while the fourth serves to knit the whole together —and in this intention it succeeds. That it breaks the accepted canons of quartet writing to a far greater extent than does the Debussy in the use of so-called orchestral effects cannot be denied, but it comes off in performance, and if that can be said of a work with any degree of truth, that work must be held to have achieved its end. It is easy to listen to for the reasons named, and only those whose attitude is that of the strict purist can object to it.

As we have remarked, it may be a matter of regret that Ravel did not write a second Quartet after the Sonata for violin and cello. Quartet writing is largely a labour of love for the composer. He can never expect to get vociferous applause or fabulous performing fees. Chamber music has a limited appeal (at the moment) and seems to be settled as the favourite form of the enlightened few. The situation is hardly brilliant, although not quite as black as the well-known composer said when asked why he did not write a string quartet: 'If I write it, no one will publish it. If it is published no one will buy it. No one will perform it. If it *is* performed no one will come to hear it. If they come to hear it, no one will like it—so why bother?' This seems an extreme case!

In considering *Introduction and Allegro* we must from the very first dismiss from our minds the thought that this is anything but a work for harp solo with accompaniment for string quartet, flute and clarinet. If we get this firmly rooted in our outlook, the work will not show up what otherwise we might regard as weaknesses. It is not chamber music in which the various instruments have independent lines contrapuntally woven together. For this reason it must be approached, not from the point of view of chamber music on the old classical and traditional lines, but from that of a pleasing and exceedingly lovely series of sounds.

Truth to tell, from the constructional point of view it has little to commend it. Ravel seems to have indulged his habit of repetition to its fullest degree. There is no development of material whatsoever and although the form is perfectly clear and easy to follow, nothing grows out of itself or out of anything we hear. It is simply statement and restatement. For this reason the purist may object that it does not conform to the canons of chamber music and, therefore, is not to be taken seriously. We disagree with this theory. There is room in the realm of chamber music for works which do not have their roots in thematic working-out or in cerebral devices which titillate the eye at the expense of the ear. It is, literally, a series of lovely sounds, and this justifies the means.

Introduction and Allegro

The Introduction really does introduce the material: the first six bars contain the germ of the whole work. It also shows off the Ravel string technique and characteristic of doubling a theme at the octave below which was formulated in the Quartet and later reached its zenith in the piano Trio.

The opening theme is in two distinct parts:

Ex. 68

'A' seems to have an oriental flavour about it which the sensuousness of 'B' takes up—at least, so it appeared to the producer of the B.B.C. serial play *The Man Born to be King*, for the whole theme was used to open and close each number, together with a later passage where a derivative of 'A' is used over a *pizzicato* bass. The effect of this application of an originally conceived piece of abstract music was quite remarkable.

The themes are restated after an effective arpeggio passage on the harp, in inversion—'A' is at the bottom while 'B' is at the top—after which an entirely new theme makes its solitary appearance underneath the Ravel paraphernalia of string arpeggios and detached arpeggio figures of the flute and clarinet. The theme in question, however, ends with a rocking three-crotchet figure —B♭, A♮, B♭—which Ravel brings to a position of unexpected importance later in the work. The Introduction leads straight into the Allegro.

This is entirely for harp solo for some number of bars, the theme being a derivative of 'B.' The flute then takes over the tune, moving above a tremolo on clarinet, viola and cello, and a *pizzicato* violin arpeggio figure. After some considerable repetition of this tune a short connecting episode, based on the concluding notes of the Introduction, leads us, with a certain amount of apparent difficulty (for the music hangs about in an unnecessary manner), to what we might term the second subject. This is unashamedly a harp tune with string accompaniment. The accompaniment bases itself on 'A' over a *pizzicato* cello and second violin, the viola doubling the tune at the octave. This two-bar phrase appears no less than five times, without variation. The harp theme is a derivative of 'B.'

Once more the connecting episode figure appears, to lead on to a four-bar phrase which is an extension of the three notes of this episode. Ravel does nothing with it for some while, but a point of interest arises when he gives the viola an augmented version of 'B.' This fragment of 'B' is hammered at in triplets of quavers and with this repetition we reach a short cadenza for the harp which, with the usual and inevitable *glissandi* and harmonics, uses 'B' as its basis. We then proceed to the re-capitulation section with the opening idea of the Allegro moving through a combined *tremolo* on all the string instruments except the cello.

'B' is thus used more extensively than ever—never once do we strike 'A' again. The connecting episode comes in again, followed by the previous expansive idea, which brings the work to a close with a *glissando* on the harp in double fifths.

That is all one can say about the work. Its absence of develop-ment is its disappointing feature; the metamorphosis of the themes is no more than any average composer could think of; but the Ravel individuality and quality are in existence in the *finesse* of the whole work, the manner of using the instruments, the exquisite polish of the ideas, the superb attention to detail.

Probably he did not intend to give the world anything but a bag of sweets, and it is something to be grateful for that his genius did not flinch before such slight ideas and such ravishing sounds as make up this little work. It has all the attributes of a musical and sensitive soul and in spite of its charm and sensuousness it is never sensual or lascivious, and these elements might quite easily have slipped in with an instrumental medium of this nature. There are those who maintain that they can see these elements in this work; surely such a basis would have entailed more deliberate continuity and note-spinning, more melodic winding and warmer harmony. We think of all the music which has this background, and then we compare it with the *Introduction and Allegro—Tristan*, the symphonies of Tchaikovsky, the concertos of Rakhmaninov (especially the second, in C minor), Skriabin's *Poem of Ecstasy*—the point is obvious.

In connection with the *Trois Poèmes de Mallarmé* we remember that in 1913 Ravel was staying at Clarens, where Stravinsky showed him Schoenberg's *Pierrot lunaire*. Ravel was struck with the possibilities of chamber music for voice and a handful of instruments, and Schoenberg's work impressed him very strongly. He determined to enrich French chamber music with a work on similar lines, the principal feature being the use of the voice in the *ensemble* rather than in solo with accompaniment. For this purpose he chose three poems by Mallarmé: *Soupir, Placet futile, Surgi de la croupe et du bond*. The instruments required are piccolo, flute, clarinet, bass clarinet and string quartet.

A composer may take a model, but it is not necessary that it be more than a model in nature. It would have been altogether impossible for Ravel to write music on the cerebral systems of Schoenberg and his followers, and although the study of *Pierrot lunaire* gave him an insight into contrapuntal possibilities, they were foreign to his natural inspiration. He imposed them upon his technique, with happy results, for in no place do we feel that the pendulum swings suddenly in the opposite direction. Curiously enough, certain passages *look* like Schoenberg—that is to say, at first glance and not knowing the composer, one might hazard a guess at central Europe. This only happens for a bar or two, and then the true Ravel breaks out. The music is intensely concentrated and no note is dispensable, each part having its own individuality and its own melodic line. Where the harmony is static, again it has the central European appearance of Webern and his researches in timbres.

Curiously enough in the same year Debussy also set three of Mallarmé's poems, including *Soupir* and *Placet futile*. We shall get an interesting comparison which, far from being odious, is exceedingly illuminating.

We have seen in the chapter on Ravel's songs that he was more concerned with declamation than with purity of melodic line. Although it would not be right to go as far as many commentators and maintain that in the *Trois Poèmes* he completely changed his approach, we may agree that in these settings we do see a more melodic approach than heretofore. Obviously the fact that he was contrapuntally rather than harmonically minded at the time led him in the direction of melody as opposed to plain declamation, but there are signs that the declamatory influence of the 'speech-song' principle of *Pierrot lunaire* influenced him in those lines where the emphasis is on a mode of address rather than on the expression of a sentiment.

Of the three poems the first, *Soupir*, is the one which is the purest Ravel as we have come to recognize him. In this song there appears little of the impulse of *Pierrot lunaire*. The accompaniment for the most part consists of string arpeggios in harmonics, at the end of which the writing becomes square and chordal. The voice-part moves freely and with ample curve, the quavers being joined together as in instrumental music—this characteristic is carried on throughout, as if Ravel wished to emphasize the essentially 'chamber-music' position of the singer in the *ensemble*. A use of appoggiaturas in the chromatic contradiction of a note in a chord dates us back to the earlier *Miroirs* and shows that, provided the contradiction is wide enough, no harshness or crudity result. *Soupir* contains no difficulties. The range is not great, the intervals are in no way difficult of approach and the general impression is of a song not remarkable for its originality although containing all the elements of its composer.

The approach to the second poem, *Placet futile*, is very different.

Here we have the essence, in many ways, of *Pierrot lunaire* in that its influence is plain in the lay-out of the scoring. A passage of scoring like this:

Ex. 69

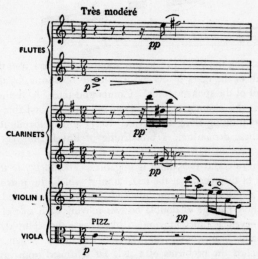

puts us immediately in mind of central Europe, while the following piano passage (which serves as an interlude in the song) seems to have some kind of system behind it.

Ex. 70

In this song the voice-part jumps about a good deal, and the rise
and fall of the notes is dictated, rather too obviously, by the rise
and fall of the spoken words. Compound intervals, diminished
octaves, the cleanest of articulation on articulate syllabic semiquavers running along a line (mercifully) of no difficulty in itself
—all these demonstrate a broadening of Ravel's inherent sense
of the combination of melody and declamation. Yet none of
it is abstruse and everything is singable. The fidelity to the demands of the accents of the text, around which the instruments
weave a spell of contrapuntal delicacy, interrupted now and again
by a short passage of double octaves moving each side of static
thirds—even at times moving in block sevenths, complete with
third and fifth—shows the extreme care with which Ravel
approached the problems of a style far separated from his own
from all points of view and the impossibility he found of severing
himself from certain characteristics which had by then (1913)
become part and parcel of his musical vocabulary. It may be
said that any composer who worked along the systems of such a
mannered thinker as Schoenberg could, with ease, turn out music
mistakable for that of 'The Master' because the system is top
priority. Ravel, however, was quite incapable of stepping into
even one shoe without speedily making it fit his own foot, no
matter how different in shape the feet of the respective owners
might have been. *Placet futile* is a monumental song, written
with the greatest attention to every detail, verging on realms outside the composer's natural territory, yet never overlapping into
the foreign one.

It may be that he felt the danger of flirting with other men's minds, because the third song, *Surgi de la croupe et du bond,* is more in the nature of the first in its static and chordal moments. The piano chords hang about a great deal while the voice-part covers the ground in a kind of natural recitative. The difficulties of intonation, etc., which characterized *Placet futile* are absent and, instead, we are faced with a melodic line of semitonal quality which spreads itself on the last bar but five, otherwise confining itself to a central point that restricts the range to the limit of an octave—we hold that for this vocal purpose D♯ is the same sound as E♭.

The first song is dedicated to Igor Stravinsky, with whom, it will be remembered, Ravel was staying at the time he first made the acquaintance of *Pierrot lunaire,* the second to Florent Schmitt, the composer's doughty champion in the days of the early riots, and the third to the inimitable Erik Satie, whose progressive ideas influenced Ravel to such an enormous degree.

As has been mentioned, Debussy also set *Soupir* and *Placet futile,* and it will be instructive to make a comparison of each composer's means of approach. We will consider, side by side, one complete sentence by each composer.

First of all (to generalize) Debussy was primarily concerned with simplicity of detail, while to Ravel this was of no great importance. Debussy makes a clear statement; Ravel delivers the music almost atmospherically—the strings indeed give the impression of a long-drawn-out sigh. (We will concede the point that Debussy was limited in the respect of graphic illustration because he confined himself to the piano.) Both composers become chordal and moving at the words 'Vers l'azur attendri d'octobre pâle et pur.' Debussy takes his accompaniment high while Ravel keeps his in the lower registers. Debussy is concerned with a piano figure, while Ravel, although keeping to a strict rhythm in the first two bars, follows the shape of the voice-part and doubles it at the top of the accompaniment. Debussy decorates, Ravel underlines.

Ex. 71

Dans le mouvt: d'un Menuet lent (♩ = 56)   Debussy

Princes - se !   à ja-lou - ser le destin d'une Hébé. Qui

poind sur cet - te tasse au bai-ser de vos lè - vres.

It is in the settings of *Placet futile* that we observe the greatest
difference of thought. It will be seen that while Ravel declaims
the line over a sustained chord (for the most part) Debussy sees
it in a quasi-recitative style. Debussy emphasizes a clear-cut
rhythm (not without traces of a Spanish influence, hardly that of
a minuet) and is content with square block-chords. Ravel, on
the other hand, gets his instrumental part moving cumulatively
until it reaches its climax, and this instrumental climax overlaps
the end of the sung sentence. Thus the music maintains movement and continuity, and proceeds from thought to thought, from
line to line, without hesitation. Debussy indulges in practically
unbroken conjunct motion, the widest leaps being three repetitions
of a third—Bb to G—and a final fourth—G to D. Debussy

Ex. 72

lowers his emphasis on the last syllable of the word 'lèvres,' while Ravel makes the word itself the climax by means of a leap of a seventh—D to C. Debussy uses the mute 'e' at the end of 'princesse'; Ravel ignores it, taking the second syllable up instead of down. The general plan of Debussy seems to have been to cover the ground without pause and to demand quick articulations of the short syllables. Ravel lingers and spreads himself, changing the whole spirit of the song with the piano interlude (Ex. 70) and following it immediately with an exceedingly flowered and decorated pianism which intermingles with the vocal line and will tend to swamp it unless considerable care is exercised to preserve the balance of parts. One would say that Debussy used the text because he wished to write a song, whereas Ravel was impelled to it for itself. The one is simple to a degree, the other ornate and decorative. Debussy lets the text speak for itself; Ravel accentuates and underlines it. Debussy has a surprising perfect cadence in E♭ at the words 'ni de rouge,' emphasizing them unduly, because the actual phrase of the words carries on to 'ni jeux mièvres'—it has led from 'ni la pastille.' Ravel makes the sentence continuous and emphasizes neither 'pastille,' 'rouge' nor 'jeux mièvres.'

It is with interest that we quote Mr. Edward Lockspeiser's remarks from his book on Debussy in the present 'Master Musicians' series. This is what he says:

. . . the slow, minuet-like accompaniment for the porcelain princess (*Placet futile*) would sound admirable if played in another room while the singer declaimed her charged and abstruse lines in a manner not very different from Schoenberg's 'Sprechsingen.'

Mr. Lockspeiser suggests that to set 'Mallarmé's later poetry, which intends to be so much music itself, was audacious if not to say superfluous.' We offer no comment on this point.

It looks as though if this poem had to be set to music, whether such an act be audacious or superfluous, or not, Ravel had got the right idea. It is a pity that Mr. Lockspeiser does not comment on Debussy's setting of *Soupir*.

Placet futile as set by Ravel can be written down as one of the greatest achievements of French vocal art, and the set of three as a whole would exercise an enormous influence on composers if only singers could perform it with any frequency.

The Trio for piano, violin and cello was composed during the early part of the 1914–19 war when Ravel was trying without success to get into the fighting services. There was little doing in the musical world to distract him and he was living very quietly, awaiting the call which eventually came—but not before he had finished the Trio. The authorities told him that he was serving France by writing music; from a certain point of view the authorities were right. From the angle of Ravel's innermost feelings they were decidedly wrong, but in writing this great Trio he certainly did serve France and the rest of the world as well.

It would not be right to say that this work came out of the war, although Ravel was affected mentally and spiritually by the catastrophe. The work had progressed far enough for the ideas to have settled themselves in his mind by the time of the German invasion—we shall see in the last chapter how he went to work when composing.

If the charge of slightness is levelled against Ravel, those who do so cannot know this Trio. Granted that the substance of the Quartet and the *Introduction and Allegro* is slender; into the Trio he put a lot of accumulated solidity which other composers seem to call into play only when dealing with the orchestra—not that the texture of the Trio is in any way orchestral either in feeling or expression.

A point which strikes us even during a cursory glance at the work is the absence of the pianism which characterized *Miroirs, Jeux d'eau* and *Gaspard de la nuit*. He seems to have exhausted these possibilities in his mind and, instead of the usual finger-muddlings, the writing is direct and full, often going on to three staves, a common device with French composers. It is said that as his model he took the Saint-Saëns Trio in F major, Op. 18, but this must not imply that one can find any outward influences of that composer. Clarity was the hall-mark of Saint-Saëns, an attribute which even those who dislike his style and idiom have to admit is above criticism. Now and again in the first movement we come across pianism which reminds us slightly of the habits in the 'grand manner' where the hands reiterate passages in broken octaves, one note in each hand, by the way, but this does not give the movement as a whole any atmosphere of grandiloquence or portentousness.

His time-signature is 8–8, an unusual measure of common time. Rhythmically this is perfectly plain and the general division of the beats is like this: The unit, therefore, is the quaver, and this moves over an ordinary bass, very largely a pedal-point, grouped in the ordinary way. Thus he obtains a charming swaying effect which flows with ease and continuity despite the crotchet of the last beat of every bar which is relieved by the division of this last beat into two quavers in the left hand. The writing is chordal for the first twelve bars, in which the piano first announces the gentle theme and is then joined by the string instruments in parallel rhythm and playing at the fifteenth. The piano fills up the intervening gap:

Ex. 73

The first evidence of the search for clarity appears immediately at the close of this passage where the cello plays the theme, high up, over an arpeggio figure of astonishing simplicity. One almost looks twice to believe one's eyes, for composers had eschewed such things:

Ex. 74

A disturbed passage brings in the connecting episode, consisting of the pianism referred to above under a scampering of reiterated semiquavers for violin and cello which leads us to an emphatic statement of the principal subject:

Ex. 75

Follows the second subject, a gentle and suave tune in Ravel's diatonic manner, punctuated by gentle chords on the piano. The tune is treated canonically for a brief bar or so by the strings:

Ex. 76

A muttering of the principal subject announces the codetta and the middle section becomes slightly turbulent with its florid right-hand piano-part, the strings referring quietly to the principal subject, the left hand continuing its deep mutterings the while.

The pace increases with corresponding intensity of feeling and the short middle section comes to an end with the idea expressed in the connecting episode. This links up with the re-entry of the principal subject, varied, itself leading on to the second subject without more ado. The coda, like the codetta, is based on the principal subject in muttering octaves under strong harmonies, the strings lingering, as it were, with gentle quavers. The music loses itself and the final six bars are marked by the rhythm of the principal subject on the lowest C of the piano.

Reference has been made to the swaying effect which characterizes this movement, and it is not without interest to note that Ravel changes his metronome markings frequently to assist the progress of the normally swaying rhythm. The unit at the beginning is 132. At the thirteenth bar it moves on to 144. Four and a half bars later he increases it to 192. Ten bars later on it is reduced to 176, while the second subject swings back to 122, and through 100 arrives at the codetta at 112. The slowest of all is 80 at the final entry of the second subject. This testifies to the extreme care Ravel exercised in his editing, a feature which has already been emphasized in the chapter on the piano works.

The second movement is called *Pantoum*. Edwin Evans tells us that it is

a form of poem which is of Malay origin but was made known in France by Ernest Fouinet and adopted by Victor Hugo in his *Orientales*. It was afterwards used by many other poets including Théodore de Banville. There is an amusing example in Austin Dobson's *At the Sign of the Lyre*. The pantoum consists of four-line stanzas from each of which the second and fourth lines are repeated as the first and third of the next. To complete the circle the last stanza repeats the second and fourth line of the opening one.[1]

The main feature is a terse figure which comes in both thematically and accompanimentally, and is followed, immediately after its initial announcement, by the main theme:

[1] From programme note to concert. 16th January 1928.

Ex. 77

The writing is clear and arpeggio-like, another amazing instance of Ravel's simplicity and slenderness.

The trio section is different. Under a ceaseless chattering of the figure in Ex. 77 'A' in triple time, the piano has a burst of chordal writing which seems to step straight out of a symphony by one of the Franckists. These composers had a habit of accumulating a climax in a chorale of triumph, an offering to the spiritual side of their inspiration to which the music seems to be striving. This is so foreign to Ravel that one wonders if at that moment he placed his tongue in his cheek and had a sly revenge for the insults of the Schola Cantorum in the early days of the *Histoires naturelles*. True, the influence does not last for long and Ravel, although keeping to the spirit, writes a harmonic succession which would have caused the Franckists great pain and tribulation. The resultant combination of this theme with the string figure— the former is *alla breve* and the latter 3-4—is visual rather than aural, but it makes a pretty picture on paper:

Ex. 78

Needless to say the parts are interchanged and the strings have the *alla breve* theme while the piano scintillates about with an elaboration of the figure. The movement finds its conclusion in pages of breath-taking delicacy alternating with vigour.

The third movement goes to the classical *Passacaille* for its frame. The theme is not treated literally note for note *ad infinitum* and *ad nauseam*, but on its third appearance is varied by repetition, thus acquiring extension and avoiding the monotony which invariably accompanies the form. The theme is spacious:

Ex. 79

Its climax is reached chordally, and the slow-moving music attains a dignity and poise which, over a swaying bass octave passage, is most moving:

Ex. 80

This movement breathes a philosophy of calm and tranquillity. It is the music of a mind at rest, quietly awaiting an inevitability with composure and resignation. It is on a broad scale, and the ending, which, like that of the first movement, gradually fades away into nothing, gives us a view as of a sun gently settling down beneath the horizon. We are left with easy minds and with assurances—but not for long, because without a break the strings dash into the *Final*, the violin playing arpeggios in harmonics and the cello a double *tremolando*.

The piano announces the theme, clear as crystal, incisive and clean-cut. This theme is in two parts. The first is chordal, with open fifths and octaves.

Ex. 81

The second part is warmer, smoother, and the icy glitter of the first part thaws into nothingness in contrast:

Ex. 82

The strings indulge in *tremolandi* quite contrary to the accepted canons of chamber-music writing, but extremely effective and not a little ominous. (For exact performance of this second part a piano with three pedals is essential, but is not often available.) The strings take up the melos, the violin soaring away with Ex. 81. The cello takes up a slight variant of Ex. 82, the piano having bravura arpeggio passages to be relieved with toccata-like incisiveness. Ex. 82 grows in intensity until it reaches its apex under soft right-hand piano *tremolandi*. The second subject appears under hard trills on the strings:

Ex. 83

The development section states both parts of the principal subject in single notes, then in octaves. The strings take up the parable until, in a shattering climax that takes our breath away, Ex. 84 is thundered out with terrific triumph:

Ex. 84

Thus the music progresses until the recapitulation opens with Ex. 81 over a strongly marked left hand which carries the movement along solidly. Ex. 82 is suggested in the strings, but makes its full appearance in the piano again. The second subject flaunts out its triumph and the enormous coda combines both parts of the principal subject with insistence on the first part. Finally, a hint at the exultation of the second subject, and this great work ends on a rising arpeggio from one extreme of the piano to the other in the chord of A with the sixth added.

This is a monumental work. Not only are the themes broad

but the whole is conceived on a big scale. 'A little master,' indeed! The resources of all the instruments are exploited to the fullest degree. Every string device is explored and used, and although the purist will undoubtedly complain of the *tremolandi* and harmonics, and find innumerable places to which he will point the finger of scorn and exclaim 'Stunt!' there is no gain-saying the greatness of the work and its consummate workmanship. Those who want the 'big Ravel' will find him here, in these pages. Those who prefer the gentle Ravel can delight in the first movement. We see the complete expression of Ravel's genius, the sum total of his musicality. The Trio bears comparison with the greatest. It is big without being grandiloquent or portentous. There is not one note too many. If size were everything, then it is second only to the great chamber works of Florent Schmitt—but size is not everything. It is content which matters. Many composers talk so much and say so little. Ravel talks a lot in this work and every word is of moment. It is not music for the amateur. A real performance can be given only by players with a vast musical experience.

It is a fact that the smaller the number of instruments, the harder the task becomes for the composer. Duet works like Ravel's Sonata for violin and cello do not abound: one can think of but a handful. The chief difficulty is to draw the line between cerebral counterpoint and the writing of a bass to a tune. It is easy, of course, to write page after page of contrapuntal music, all full of ingenuity in imitations, sequences, canons, etc., but devoid of any inspirational fire. The late Edwin Evans once warned composers against that dangerous 'Mr. Fugato,' the anchor of deficient inspiration. Another difficulty is to keep the work from sounding as if the pianist had failed to turn up, and the two string players were, therefore, doing their best without him. On the other hand, it would never do to attempt too much on the two string instruments, and thus give the impression of two players doing the work of four. Only a composer with complete confidence in himself can be advised to adopt such a scheme.

It will have been noticed that Ravel was subject to no 'isms,' processes or systems. He belonged to no school and propounded no principles or theories. He merely wrote music and his technique was his own individuality. We have seen in the string Quartet that he was not addicted to counterpoint *per se*. How, then, did he approach the problems attendant upon a work for two 'one-line' instruments?

It will be remembered that Stravinsky introduced him to Schoenberg's *Pierrot lunaire*, that work containing all the imaginable devices of the cerebral musician, and that Ravel was constrained to write his *Trois Poèmes de Mallarmé*, not by the suggestion of the system of Schoenberg's music, but by the unusual combination of instruments and voice. In the early 1920s snobbery was the order of the day. Composers were attempting to rid music of all its romanticism and were drawn to terse statement and economy of means. Ravel always carefully avoided getting mixed up with fashionable circles, and snobs were anathema to him. Nevertheless, he followed all the latest ideas with interest and carefully noted those which seemed to align themselves with his own thought. At this time the facility for composing was beginning to leave him, and he took longer over the present work than those of previous years. This was not entirely the result of his state of health, but was bound up with a certain feeling that he had come to a dead end and his technique and idiom were forming new paths for themselves. We have but to compare the works of this period with the preceding ones to see this. For the first time in his life he submitted himself to processes and allowed his mind to govern his natural flow of inspiration. This being so, he was undoubtedly right to discipline himself to the rigours of writing for two string instruments, and we have read of the length of time it took to complete the Sonata.

Two roads are open to the composer of this type of work. The first is to write avowedly a tune with accompaniment, the second to adhere strictly to a two-line contrapuntal system. A combination of both roads is possible only when the composer is a master of his craft. He is also faced with the problem whether his music shall go for 'effects' or shall remain 'pure' music. The ethics of chamber music would seem to forbid the former, but as long as the effects can be put inside the thematic and musical ideas, there can be no objection. Of course it must be remembered that what ten years before was considered a trick can become legitimate in due time. It is largely a matter of invention.

Ravel faced the problems boldly, and in his first movement the balance between contrapuntal treatment of the ideas and the harmonization, as it were, of a melody is admirably maintained. There is frequent use of harmonics, both in occasional notes and in arpeggio passages. The two instruments play in different keys —not accidentally, but with differing key signatures—but the parts are in no way as difficult as they look.

The work is in four movements. The first, in duple time, flows along with good continuity. It is built upon an alternation of minor and major common chords, an idea which Walton exploited in his viola Concerto. There are few resultant clashes, although the sharp and the natural are often only one quaver apart. Each line by itself is satisfactory when it is melodically conceived; in other places the thought is harmonic and slightly in the nature of an accompaniment. This is not wrong, or contrary to any exact principles, since it is incidental rather than habitual. The following passage, within its limits, illustrates this point:

Ex. 85

It is refreshing to find no self-conscious inversion of the parts. Although the cello announces the opening theme, on its return Ravel does not feel compelled to give it to the violin; and there is no evidence of deliberate contrapuntal device, no inversions of themes or augmentations and diminutions are put in to give the movement continuity and the composer a reputation for skill. All the skill of the craftsman, however, is there and is patent all through.

The second movement is the scherzo. On paper it looks curiously inept, but in performance the pace brings it off all right. A repetition of a *pizzicato* theme in the cello entirely alone, and later supported by a sustained violin note, seems to need some justification and suggests flagging of invention, with too much reliance placed upon speed. The coda, however, is very effective even if the cello does concentrate on two chords for a long time. This movement seems too easy.

A short slow movement follows which is exquisitely wrought. Ravel starts off with an eight-bar tune which suggests *fugato* treatment. Mercifully he does not fall for the obvious—in the Sonata for violin and piano we shall see how the avoidance of the obvious in this respect spoils a good thing—and the counterpoint throughout the opening subject is excellent. At the end the theme is treated with an accompanimental figure, the contrapuntal writing relieving the 'tune with accompaniment' very charmingly.

The last movement is one of those *tours de force* that make one wonder about their value. Now and again one feels that one is convinced, then something happens which points to a certain aridity. On consideration one is inclined to call this move-ment a failure, in spite of the reintroduction of previous themes.

The opening terse statement has vigour and vitality:

Ex. 86

but it goes no farther than this, and instead of expansion we have endless repetition. The alternation of minor and major appears again, but by this time we cease to notice it. It sounds as if Ravel had lost all interest in the work and finished it perfunctorily, of necessity. There is no burning flame behind it. He nearly falls

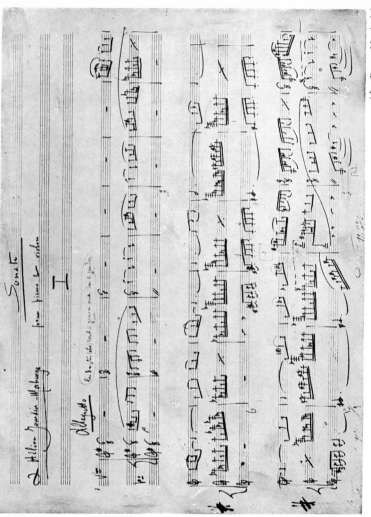

AUTOGRAPH OF SONATA FOR VIOLIN AND PIANO

into central European style and remembers his manners just in time. It may have been an experiment; certainly it is something quite new in Ravel styles—and the style does not suit him.

Only the two slow movements are at all satisfactory; only those who live on the excitements of experiment can react enthusiastically to this work by Ravel out of central Europe. No doubt the elect of the snobbish intelligentsia rejoiced to find that Ravel was at last 'up to date.' In an otherwise pleasant garden this Sonata stands out as an arid patch.

Whatever failings the last work may have had, they were eradicated in the Sonata for violin and piano, where Ravel seems perfectly at home. Not being a contrapuntist by nature, he found the piano a safe sheet-anchor, and his love of sonorities found its true level with this instrument. It is strange that he waited so long before delivering himself of a work of this nature. His maturity had passed through the refining fire, and after the aridity and sterility of the Sonata for violin and cello he found himself again in the more congenial surroundings of violin and piano.

This work is in three movements, the second of which is in the form of a 'Blues.' Ravel declared himself to be rather attracted to the jazz of the period, an ominous sign, for his sense of rhythm never needed any lesson from this realm of 'music.'

The first movement opens with a widely spacing subject on the piano, entirely unadorned with chords or frills. When the violin takes it up we have been led to expect *fugato* writing, and it is here that the avoidance of the obvious spoils a good thing. The theme, instead of moving along still farther, goes back on its tracks and becomes immobile over a synthetic movement of semiquaver octave *tremolo* on B♭. However, since Ravel chose to avoid the obvious, let us admit that possibly it would have been either dull or calculated had he attempted something contrary to his natural bent. This movement reveals all the charm of the composer's genius. It is gentle music flowing with an easy grace. A fondness for open fifths again sounds better than it looks on paper, and generally speaking the slender texture of the piano writing is refreshing. If anything, the movement suffers from repetition, a failing which we first noticed in the string Quartet, and one which perhaps justifies detractors in considering him incapable of sustained development. Remembering M. D. Calvocoressi's dictum on this subject, we hesitate to ascribe it to weakness of technique.

Of the 'Blues' perhaps the best testimony is in the statement of a dance-band leader of international fame whom I took to a performance of the work at one of the concerts of the R.A.M. New Music Society. He described it as the most perfect 'Blues' he had ever heard, because it conveyed exactly the nostalgia of the dance and was perfectly constructed. It was, he said, a true 'Blues,' not necessarily to be danced to any more than we dance to Chopin's waltzes, but to steep oneself in. He was surprised that its composer should have stayed 'in the serious music racket.'

The essence of the 'Blues' is deep depression and nostalgia, obtained with a monotonous rhythm of repeated chords in regular square metre. Ravel's tune consists of long rather than short notes, and its range is strictly limited. In the middle the piano takes up an entirely new pattern:

Ex. 87

but the violin pursues its slow and long-noted tune. Later we get an inner melody underneath the repeated B. Since we have the above authority for stating this movement's value as a 'Blues,' we would not gainsay it, but will restrict ourselves to saying that it is deeply moving.

All the musical interest lies in the piano in the last movement, a 'Perpetuum mobile.' The violin has groups of swiftly moving semiquavers and literally nothing else. This is really exciting music and the 'perpetual motion' is in no way artificial. It is all of a piece and the piano simply pursues a quiet path of considerable strength. It certainly is not in the sonata tradition; indeed the work is so fresh and individual that it stands by itself. Ravel told his interpreter that 'it will not be difficult.' Ask violinists if he was right. However, the difficulty or otherwise of any work does not concern us here. We face a Sonata of great originality, not particularly deep in thought or broad in conception, but individual to its composer and an ornament for a repertory which includes far too much that is commonplace.

CHAPTER XII

THE OPERAS

RAVEL'S two operas, *L'Heure espagnole* and *L'Enfant et les sorti-lèges*, are unique. Without in any way setting out to write either *opéra bouffe* or *opéra comique*, Ravel succeeds in combining the elements of both, at the same time showing an innate skill in the handling of dramatic situations, even if those situations are not very dramatic from the point of view from which such a feature is usually regarded. It would have been quite impossible for him to take a serious opera seriously, and it may well have been that the abortive works which we have mentioned became so be-cause he knew within himself that such subjects were not really within his scope. It is a psychological fact that creative artists of all kinds harbour secret longings to express themselves in modes and manners outside their natural range and capacity, probably because there is a subconscious sense of frustration and restriction. That Ravel should have attempted things like *Shéhérazade* and *Mor-giana* is, therefore, in the natural order of things, and so is the fact that he should have given up both ideas. We may be grateful that he did so, because they might have succeeded, in which case we might not have had the two individual operas that were com-pleted. Once a composer with dramatic leanings succeeds in one field, that is the end of his normal progress. We would not be without one of the two operas in question. *L'Heure espagnole* has been performed in this country; *L'Enfant et les sortilèges* has so far not been given us. The reason is not difficult to find. The former is an entertaining fifty-odd minutes of intrigue which is a reality. The latter is not real, and the work itself is not simple enough in the way that *Hänsel und Gretel* is simple. It is not a pantomime and it is not a serious opera. To our feeling, the child's adventures fall between two stools. We shall see that the score of *L'Enfant et les sortilèges* is unexciting and extremely economical. Further, somehow or other French children do not appeal to us in any way. If this work were to succeed in this country the music would have to be definite enough thematically to enable the tunes to hang about our ears. As it is, they are not of that quality, and the whole work is too declamatory. Nevertheless, it can take its place among European operas and stand on its own legs in its own surroundings.

There are those who have a distaste for opera as a species because it is irrational and absurd when it takes itself seriously. These people have a rooted objection to operatic heroes who puff out their chests and say what fine fellows they are; they object to the blood-and-thunder type of work which has done duty as a representation of the true operatic style. Nevertheless, they are willing to concede that when the opera in question has entertainment value, when it deliberately sets out to be picturesque and amusing, even if serious in certain of its aspects, then it has its place in their affection. Such a work is *L'Heure espagnole*. It is witty, naughty, sparkling, intriguing and entirely lacking in the operatic traditions. There are no opportunities for vocal acrobatics although the voice-parts are not just plain and easy lines. Scenically it offers opportunities in a small way. The libretto is a good libretto to read and it is based on an everyday escapade which is familiar in every country. Most favourable aspect of all, the music has scintillation and colour, piquancy and melody in its somewhat limited range, and its roots lie in a country whose musical traditions are well known and well liked.

The scene of *L'Heure espagnole* is laid in a Spanish clock-shop owned by Torquemada, who has an attractive wife, Concepcion. Before the curtain rises there is a prelude in which we hear all manner of clocks chiming simultaneously. There is a cuckoo clock, one with an automatic cock-crow, a musical box and other delightful models. All these happen over an accompaniment chordal in nature and continuously moving. The curtain rises during this prelude.

Ramiro, a government muleteer, brings his watch, a family heirloom, to be repaired. It has suddenly stopped and he is unable to carry out his official duties with his mules if he does not know the time. Torquemada examines it and while he does so Concepcion calls him. Why is he still at home? Does he not realize that it is the day on which he puts all the municipal clocks in Toledo right? Torquemada, to the complete astonish- ment of Ramiro, asks her what the time is—pointing out that no clockmaker ever looks at his own clocks. Concepcion bustles him off, to the distress of Ramiro who needs his watch and has been told by Torquemada to wait in the shop till he returns.

Concepcion is delighted that at last it is her 'day off' from her husband, and that she is free to do exactly what she wants. Ramiro is rather embarrassed, for he never knows what to say to women, and here he is with a perfectly charming one and quite unable to leave before his watch is put right. Concepcion shows him some fascinating clocks, especially one which she says has to be moved but is far too heavy for her. Ramiro offers to carry it up to her room for her. She is astonished at his boldness. She wanted to ask him to do so, but did not dare, etc. Ramiro gallantly replies that every muleteer is at heart 'un reménageur amateur.' Concepcion is all confusion, but Ramiro reassures her. He is only too pleased to have something to do since it will remove the strain of trying to find something to say. He places the clock on his shoulder and goes out.

At the same moment the voice of Gonsalve, a bachelor, is heard outside. There is 'a thing' between him and Concepcion. He is delighted that once more *his* day of freedom with Concepcion has come round again and the jealous husband is away. He is very verbose, and Concepcion reminds him that time is short and that he had better cut the cackle. Gonsalve, however, is full of his own words and nothing Concepcion can do will stop their flow. Concepcion is fearful lest the muleteer should overhear Gonsalve or come down and catch them unawares. Gonsalve, however, is a poet at heart and is mindful of only one thing—

Gonsalve; hence when Ramiro really does appear he takes him as a matter of course, but is astonished that a muleteer is able to talk. Concepcion is anxious to get Ramiro out of the way and tells him that after all she thinks the clock which he carried upstairs would be better in the shop. Ramiro is perfectly willing to move it anywhere, as by so doing he will fill up still more time. He accordingly goes upstairs again. Concepcion is afraid lest Ramiro will give her away because he has the evil eye. However, she suddenly hits upon a plan. When he comes down again with the first clock, she will ask him to carry another one up to her room, and this clock will contain Gonsalve. Gonsalve with a poetical flourish goes inside the grandfather clock and Concepcion shuts the door.

At that moment the voice of Don Inigo Gomez, a banker, is heard, greeting Concepcion. He, too, is taking advantage of the day that Torquemada is out, winding up the municipal clocks. Concepcion is uneasy. What with Ramiro upstairs and Gonsalve inside a clock, goodness knows what will happen. She begs Inigo to speak quieter—'Clocks have ears.' He presses his suit rather too ardently for Concepcion's comfort, and at the crucial moment Ramiro comes down with the clock. Concepcion warns him that the other will be very heavy, but Ramiro is tough. He passes the clock from one shoulder to the other with the utmost nonchalance, to the distress of Gonsalve and of Concepcion, who is afraid that harm will come to him. She offers to go upstairs with Ramiro, saying that the mechanism is very fragile. Don Inigo is offended at being left alone, and determines to have his revenge by hiding; so he goes inside another clock and pulls the door to.

Ramiro comes down. He is charmed with Concepcion—why, she has actually asked him to mind the shop in her absence upstairs. He ruminates upon the comparison of women and mechanism, both very fragile and unreliable. Concepcion enters in a great state. The words stick in her throat. She has suddenly realized that she cannot sleep in her room with a ticking and chiming clock. Ramiro is only too ready to oblige with another removal, and goes off upstairs again.

Don Inigo inside the clock imitates the cuckoo. Concepcion feels that it is out of place and in bad taste to make a noise like a cuckoo under the circumstances. Don Inigo comes out of the clock. He is quite proud of his achievement in making Concepcion think that the clock really did 'cuckoo.' Wait and see what he will be able to do with a little practice! Conception begs him to go, but Don Inigo is a poet like Gonsalve. He appeals to Concepcion, as a poet. She capitulates.

At that moment Ramiro comes down with the clock containing Gonsalve. Concepcion pushes Don Inigo back into his clock and asks Ramiro to carry it up to her room. He obliges cheerfully and willingly.

Concepcion taunts Gonsalve in his clock and lets him out, asking him to go. She puts him off by telling him that he can recite his couplets as much as he likes; she has had enough of them, and she shuts him back in his clock. Gonsalve is not a whit abashed. He sings heartily in his clock to himself. Ramiro re-enters. He is well pleased with himself. Concepcion is charming, the shop is charming, nothing disturbs him. He has nothing to say and nothing to think. The clocks begin to chime and Ramiro is enchanted by them. He decides that if he were not a muleteer he would like to be the owner of this clock-shop.

Concepcion catches his words and interrupts. Ramiro inquires if there is anything still wrong with the clock. Is it not right yet? Very well; he will go and fetch it, and out he goes. Concepcion is tired of the whole affair. She determines to get rid of both her lovers and by so doing will be faithful to the clockmaker. Poets? Pah! She knocks on the door of Gonsalve's clock. Conveniently enough, down comes Ramiro with Don Inigo's clock on his back. He is quite ready to climb upstairs again with the first clock or with both at once. It is all the same to him. Which will the señora prefer? The señora has fallen for Ramiro's unconscious charms. These poets may be all right, but give her a *man*. Ramiro again asks which clock he is to carry up. Will he please go up into her room—and without either clock. The invitation is accepted.

The two poets are left inside their clocks. Don Inigo pokes his head out and finds no one present. He is annoyed. He makes a fuss, calling for the door to be opened. The door slams on him, at the noise of which Gonsalve pokes his head out of his clock. He sings a long farewell to his clock—his prison, his helmet, his breastplate, his cage. While so occupied, he perceives Torquemada returning. Don Inigo appears in his clock. Torquemada is delighted at finding customers waiting for him even if they are inside his clocks. They sing the praises of Torquemada's watches and clocks. Indeed, the time spent in waiting for him has passed very pleasantly. Torquemada says that curiosity is natural and that of course they may look inside the clocks. Torquemada sells Don Inigo his clock, and in order that Gonsalve may not be jealous, sells him his for the same price. They both ask to be released from their clocks. Don Inigo suddenly sees Ramiro and Concepcion. He calls Ramiro, and Torquemada remembers that hours ago he had promised to mend Ramiro's watch. Inigo cannot get out of his clock, so Ramiro picks him out with one hand. Torquemada is not sure about Ramiro, but Concepcion tells him that regular as a clock Ramiro passes with his mules, each morning, under her window, and Torquemada asks him to call out the time every day. The quintet addresses the public with a moral on conjugal fidelity, which novel ending brings down the curtain.

This altogether charming and amusing plot offered Ravel every possible opportunity for his Hispanicism. It has been said that a Spanish composer would not have been so wholesale in his use of Spanish rhythms and dances, but Ravel was always prepared to outmode the fashion and outdo the native. He introduces several Spanish national features into this work—Gonsalve's arietta is in the form of a *malagueña* and the concluding quintet in that of a *habanera*.

There are no set arias or *ensemble* numbers. The music is carried on continuously in conversation form, not of the nature of *Pelléas et Mélisande*, but in a style infinitely more definite and clearer drawn. There is regular metre between his orchestra and voices, and the orchestra never hangs about while the voices deliver *recitativo parlando*. The conversation is metrical.

The Spanish touches are genuine and part of the work. Except for the closing quintet, it is seldom that any of the dance movements is carried to a conclusive ending. However, the best points of the work lie in the ingenious chiming of the clocks and the combination of tones. It is, of course, perfectly easy to make forty clocks chime all at once, provided that the resultant sound does not matter. In this case, the dissonances and sonorities are organized sufficiently to make them sound natural and yet spontaneous and logical. The whole score might have been written with a fine needle. It is as neat in construction as Ravel himself was neat in appearance.

L'Enfant et les sortilèges also has a domestic moral, but one directed not at conjugal infidelity and all its serious imports, but at child behaviour. No sermon is intended in either work, but the 'lessons' are there. In the first place, wives must behave themselves or they may land in situations over which they will have little control. Children must be good or their best friends (their toys) will rise against them—and that would be terrible.

There is almost nothing to say about this work. The story may be summarized very briefly in the statement that a child behaves badly, whereupon all his nursery furniture and his toys become animated and express their disgust. As they get out of hand, the child decides that he had better be good, and the opera ends with the child's plaintive cry 'Maman!' That is all.

Musically one might say that it is a marvel of economy. Page after page shows us the voice-part accompanied by one or two instruments only. Very rarely is there anything which we can take out of the score and consider as a 'set number.' There is very little of the kind in *L'Heure espagnole*, but there we have at least action and situations. In *L'Enfant et les sortilèges* nothing is real. The sight of two chairs dancing together may be quaint, but it is not very funny. The cats and the other live elements are very well drawn in effect, but they are not music. Ravel took a long time over this work. Was he bored with it? He probably enjoyed making the 'funny noises' on the orchestra, but was that at the back of his mind? Of invention as it is known and understood in symphonic music there is none. Of invention in the sense of ingenuity there is plenty, but we do not go to the opera or to the concert-hall to hear funny noises, no matter how ingenious.

The only moment where there is any continuity is in the fox-trot *Five o'Clock*, which is typical of its kind, but not what one would expect to hear from a composer like Ravel. However, composers do enjoy a night out in alien fields at times, and Ravel probably felt refreshed after the experiment.

This work is the only disappointing one in the whole of Ravel's output. Perhaps it is that we are not made that way. The objections to it from our point of view have been stated earlier in the chapter. With infinite regret one must confess that *L'Enfant et les sortilèges* is dull.

CHAPTER XIII

RAVEL AS WRITER FOR ORCHESTRA

IT is a revealing fact that for the concert hall Ravel wrote precisely one originally scored work, with the addition of the piano concertos. This is surprising, since it is so very easy to think of him as an essentially orchestral composer. The other works we hear are either stage works or transcriptions of piano pieces and suites. These transcriptions were made mainly by Ravel himself and, therefore, they have full authority for their existence.

Considering this subject, we find that only the *Rapsodie espagnole* exists as an intended concert-hall work, and is, it will be remembered, an early effort, comparatively speaking. True, *La Valse* was conceived as a kind of symphonic poem glorifying Vienna, and had the original title *Wien*, but Ravel turned it into a choreographic poem for Ida Rubinstein. This need not deter us from considering him as an orchestral writer, even though we may be inclined to think of him as an 'orchestrator.' We must remember *Daphnis et Chloé* and the piano concertos. None of these, of course, were ever meant to be played as piano works, even though the first exists in a piano version, any more than *L'Heure espagnole* or *L'Enfant et les sortilèges*.

Roland-Manuel, as we have read, considers the *Rapsodie espagnole* a 'study for orchestra,' and we may rightly agree with him. Into it Ravel put all the nuances and experiments in orchestral timbres that he could think of. It is one effect after another, but no one can blame him, because he attempted to paint four pictures of Spain. The extreme delicacy of the scoring defies criticism, but not everybody finds the approach acceptable. Cecil Gray says:

The element which one most dislikes in Ravel's music, however, is his orchestration, which reveals the influence of the Russians, and of Rimsky-Korsakov in particular, in the constant preoccupation with

external brilliance and meretricious glitter. He relies to a quite dis-
proportionate extent on what one might call the confectionery department of the orchestra—harp 'glissandi,' glockenspiel and celesta. . . .
Nothing palls so quickly on the palate as this cloying sweetness. The
Rapsodie espagnole is perhaps the most extreme example of this tendency.[1]

This, of course, is tantamount to saying that a complete concert
of Ravel's works on the orchestra would be a monotonous affair.
Probably it would; but there are few composers who can pass
such a test. We do, indeed, find Ravel's *batterie* the most complete to be found in any composer. There is hardly anything
except Schoenberg's iron chains in the *Gurrelieder* which he
does not use. Whether this is a vice or a virtue depends on the
individual. If we approach Ravel in the spirit of the Teutonic
or central European school, we shall find no lines or solidity of
thought. We shall wend our way along no instrumental
wormlike paths of melody. There will be no developments or
long workings-out. But we shall find no mud: everything is
crystal-clear. In the larger works such as *Daphnis et Chloé* he
treats the orchestra as a virtuoso instrument. He realizes that the
world's finest players can do no more than merely 'play the notes'
or give the bare bones of the matter. He decorates everything.
The strings are called upon to do feats usually expected only in the
solo part of a concerto. The wind will find their resources used
to an extraordinary degree of completeness. Always we are faced
with consummate good taste, exquisite tone-painting and masterly
editorship. Mr. Myers Foggin has called attention to this in his
remarks on the piano works. In the orchestral scores we find it
developed to a complete art. Not for him the vague *crescendo*
hairpin, beginning not always quite surely and often ending
inexactly, or the careless marking of dynamics on a common level.
Each instrument is treated as if there were no others, or as if that
particular instrument were a soloist. There is nothing careless,
nothing left to chance.

The score of *Daphnis et Chloé* is as good an instruction book on

[1] *A Survey of Contemporary Music* (1924).

orchestration as any student and many mature composers could be recommended to buy. One could prescribe a course for composers with the gift of rapid and slick scoring which would consist of a minute study of *Daphnis et Chloé*, and nothing else, for a month.

It was, of course, impossible for him to be literal. Even a sustained third in the piano score brought to his mind innumerable possibilities. He visualized everything from the player's angle. Hence the pages are picturesque with string arpeggios; the strings themselves are subdivided into two and often three parts, and every note has its accent or staccato dot (see opposite page). If he writes a *glissando* on the trombones he is careful to give the position; his harp parts are 'edited' with the chromatic accidentals named as they would appear in the player's copy.

The only works in which he was at all obvious in his scoring are *Ma Mère l'Oye* and *Le Tombeau de Couperin*, that work which breathes the spirit of French classicism. The *Valses nobles et sentimentales,* too, avoid the temptation to elaborate. It is this breadth and expansiveness of thought which seem to make life too difficult. Although his scoring is undoubtedly of the line of Rimsky-Korsakov, Ravel outdid the Russian composer in resource. The Russian would never split up his strings in the Ravel manner —yet his music sounds just as effective. Where Ravel would write spacious arpeggios, Rimsky-Korsakov would obtain an equally warm effect by a simple undivided *tremolando*. This must not be read as a weakness in Ravel. It was only that his point of view, one of scrupulous detail, made him specialize in the individual part as against a contemplation of the whole. If it is a virtue, Rimsky-Korsakov is easier to play than Ravel; but he is not nearly so interesting. There is less contrast in the Russian than in the Frenchman.

Ravel's care of the *batterie*, which so upsets Mr. Cecil Gray, betokens more than a mere passion for tintinnabulation. It betokens considerable enterprise and insistence on detail. Let us

Ex. 88

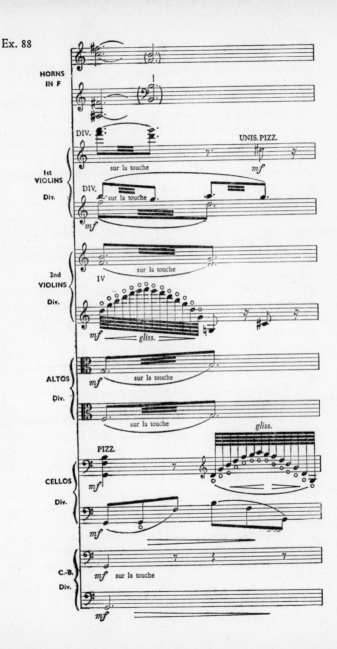

look at some of the requirements in *La Valse*, *Daphnis et Chloé* and *L'Heure espagnole*.

La Valse is deliberately flashy music. The percussion is used to lighten what would otherwise sound heavy and ponderous. The opulence of the melodic lines, far more Viennese than Vienna, makes for heaviness and too much richness. He asks for triangle, Basque drum, tambourine, castanets, Chinese gong and wood clappers. All these are legitimate and are to be found in many orchestral works, except the wood clappers which are usually relegated to other haunts. He knew exactly when to use them, and unlike the composer of recent years who emphasized every *crescendo* with a crash on the cymbals, realized that the use of these plates of metal becomes effective only when sparingly applied.

Daphnis et Chloé adds celesta, xylophone and aeoliophone to the above assortment. The last-named is a wind machine which makes but a short appearance. In case any reader should wish to explore this instrument, its notation consists of a trill above a note-head. There is no pitch. It gives an eerie sound. Strauss uses it in *Don Quixote* with a different intention, namely, that of making a noise like the wind. Ravel uses it to give simply an effect of terror and mystery to an awe-inspiring scene.

In *L'Heure espagnole* he takes the requirements farther. Here we find him encroaching on what another composer might well have left to the 'props department.' It is an essential to his production that all kinds of clocks shall all tick at once. Ravel does not leave this to chance. He scores it in his score. Thus we find three lines devoted, in all seriousness, to three pendulums meticulously metronomed at 40, 100 and 132 respectively, and he does not hesitate to indicate where each pendulum is to be stopped. In addition we have the whirr of the clock springs indicated in the score, as well as the definitely musical tinkling chimes and bird-songs. Hence the *batterie* becomes an integral part of the *mise-en-scène*, as it were.

L'Heure espagnole is a marvel of design and detail. There is the clarity which he had learned from Saint-Saëns and the impeccable good taste which characterized everything he did, and his own person.

Probably the best example of his consummate skill in using the resources of each instrument to its fullest extent is found in the orchestral version he made of Mussorgsky's *Pictures from an Exhibition*. To this work he brought a quite personal freshness of orchestral treatment. For those who find the music in its original state unconvincing and even dull Ravel provides a veritable revelation. Listening to it, one would be pardoned for thinking it an original orchestral work. Nothing is obvious and yet nothing is forced or far-fetched. He even manages to put an inquiring tone into the simple *Promenades*. Such characterization as we find in the picture of the two Jews, for example, is something which stands by itself in music. Of course Ravel had every opportunity for his favourite elaboration in this work, since the piano writing is often square and chordal. To compare the simple piano copy with Ravel's full score is indeed to make one marvel. Kussevitsky, who commissioned Ravel to do the job, knew that he was on safe ground in entrusting him with the work.

CHAPTER XIV

GENERAL SUMMARY

IT is in no way to limit his reputation to come to the conclusion that Ravel was first and foremost a writer for the piano. In this respect he leads the world among all the composers of the present century. More resourceful than Debussy, more varied and more highly skilled in using the complete range of the instrument, he brought to modernity the natural pianistic aptitude of Liszt. One has but to consider a simple piece like the familiar *Liebestraum* and compare it with the writing of the Concerto for the left hand to realize that Ravel understood the *cantabile* characteristics of a thumb-melody better than any one else. If on the one hand we have the books of *Préludes* to reveal Debussy, we have no parallel in that composer with *Gaspard de la nuit*. The poetic resources and potentialities of the piano are, in Ravel, explored to the full and there seems to be nothing left to do. In the whole range of his piano music there is only one piece to which we can point and say 'dull' or 'uninteresting' and that is the *Noctuelles* in the *Miroirs*. This is more than can be said of most composers.

The technique required to play Ravel is not an extra specialized one, in spite of the complexities which appear on the surface. He requires tidy playing and impeccable workmanship. Every note so plays its part that not even an arpeggio can be rearranged without upsetting the entire balance of the passage. His arpeggios are all in the context and do not appear as mere figuration. The fact that his piano music transfers well to the orchestra is not so remarkable as the reverse would be. Very little modern music of a romantic or efflorescent type stands the 'black-and-white test,' so firmly believed in by Sir Charles Stanford. With Ravel even the *Rapsodie espagnole* sounds well played as a piano duet, in spite of its reliance on orchestral effect. Play *L'Après-midi* on the piano and follow it by the *Rapsodie* and the difference between the two composers at once becomes obvious. Debussy's wonderful orchestral fresco sounds grey and stodgy. Ravel's coloured post-card sounds as musical as it does on the orchestra, although, of course, not so musically intentioned.

It is impossible to exaggerate the importance of Ravel as a piano writer. It is too soon for his influence to be felt because he is too near our own time. Liszt 'happened' a long time ago. Many of his tricks have become played out and we can see in them much meretricious display. Any one basing his pianism, either consciously or unconsciously, on Ravel will sound a mere reflection. This is bound to happen when a composer so highly stylized (I do not say mannered) as Ravel is so near us. Thirty years will see the effect of Ravel on piano composers as they will see the effect of Roussel on French symphonists. The matter will never fade and although at the moment no extension of the manner seems to be possible, it would not be safe to prophesy that it is a dead end.

In the realm of chamber music one doubts if he will influence future generations. The *très délicieux* and *ravissant* aspects of the Quartet and the *Introduction and Allegro*, particularly the latter, are not aspects which can be continued indefinitely. The Sonata for violin and cello is not the basic Ravel. On the other hand one must pay homage to the piano Trio, one of the greatest of all time. It is noteworthy that he wrote only one work for each medium.

As for the songs, we have seen the simplicity of the early examples, of the *Ronde* particularly, worthy to rank with Fauré's *Clair de lune* as a perfect example of the essence of the French genius. The *Trois Poèmes de Mallarmé* can rank with any songs written by any composer, and it can be only the fact that singers do not like difficulties that they are not performed more often. The *Histoires naturelles* are a great historical landmark and deserve to remain alive for this very reason, if for no other. They marked the turning of a tide.

With the orchestra he may be considered more an orchestrator than an orchestral composer. He had all the sense of the orchestra, but his innate gift of thinking in a keyboard manner precludes him from being regarded as essentially an orchestral composer; the transfer from the one medium to the other is too easy. Yet no one could score so gloriously, so richly as Ravel. It was orchestration that Vaughan Williams studied with him. Ravel 'directed my now rather polyphonic method of orchestration which I had evolved from Wagner and Strauss.' [1] The love of detail which made Ravel elaborate a single chord, his passion for divided strings, may be complex, but his motto was 'Complexe, mais pas compliqué.' [1]

We may dislike his orchestral handling much as we may dislike Botticelli, but we cannot deny its individuality and its faultless and unfailing precision. Here, again, his editing is exemplary.

Generally speaking he was not concerned with the exploitation of sonorities. The 'juxtaposition of tones' played a part only incidental to his expression. He was not concerned with this or that scale and did not make any fetish of any particular chord or chords. He was never preoccupied with a furtherance of 'textbook harmony' to the extent of regarding any one chord in the light of a common concord. Indeed, his use of common chords we have seen to be a peculiar and natural part of his technique. He had, therefore, a broader range than Debussy, who bothered too much about sonorities. Ravel did not use dominant ninths as a basis; he used them when they happened to be required. Thus his variety is far more extensive than Debussy's. We can point to several of the latter's *Préludes* and apply the term 'limited' to them; but in no single case can we do so with Ravel unless the unsympathetic like to point to the obviously monotonous effect of the pedal-point in *Le Gibet*, the regularity of which was, of course, intentional. He did not use the orchestra for tints. He used it as a mass, and his colour, though refined, is laid on thickly (paradoxical though this may seem).

When we play the *Children's Corner* we feel that Chou-chou

[1] From a letter to the author dated 16th April 1946.

Debussy must have been a sophisticated little Miss. When we play *Ma Mère l'Oye* we know that the Gobedski children really were children. Debussy sounds self-conscious. Ravel, having greater range of expression, sounds perfectly natural. When Debussy wrote a waltz it was a flimsy affair. When Ravel did the same, the result had body and personality.

His methods of composition were strange. Often he would sketch out the pages with bar lines, decide how long the phrases were to be and plan the key successions. This, before he had a single idea as to what the themes were to be. The work would evolve from this plan and his ideas would be made to fit the frame. This scheme may very well have contributed to the brevity of his middle sections and limited the scope of his thought.

As a conductor, he may be said to have been the best type of composer-conductor—he was so bad. For what he was as a pianist we may once more turn to Mr. Gordon Bryan for information:

Before Ravel arrived, a gramophone company suggested his recording *Jeux d'eau*, but knowing about his limited technical ability from Dr. Vaughan Williams, I hedged until he arrived, when he exclaimed in dismay: 'But I have never played it in my life!' His performance in the violin and piano Sonata, and his accompaniment to the songs, were vitally rhythmical and extremely authoritative in style, which is not always the case with composers. Even if not invariably accurate, it did not seem to matter—for instance, when he had written difficult arpeggios in the aria from *L'Heure espagnole*, which was sung by Odette de Foras, he played them 'glissando' with excellent effect.

I was turning over the music of the violin Sonata (which was played by Frederick Holding) and during the first movement Ravel suddenly realized that he had not put on his spectacles. Whereupon he groped in his coat-tail pocket with his right hand, meanwhile attempting to play what should be on two hands with left hand alone. When he had secured the glasses, I adjusted them on his nose, to the amusement of the nearer members of the audience, but considerably less amusement of the violinist, who had to continue as usual during this pantomime. Ravel was thoroughly unselfconscious, and indulged in many asides to me, commenting with self-satisfaction on the music and sundry harmonic progressions therein, as though we had been rehearsing in private.

M. D. Calvocoressi, who knew him intimately, gives some interesting insights into Ravel as an individual and into certain views of his music:

When one came into contact with him, the first impression was almost sure to be that of dryness and aloofness—very different from the semi-shy, semi-ironical reserve that was Debussy's first line of defence. He was endowed with a great capacity for indifference and also contempt, but—as one found out quite soon—as great a capacity for admiration; and I was to realize a little later that behind the cutting manner, the irony and the aloofness there lurked an even greater capacity for affection. . . .

Many people alleged that the care he took to exclude from his music all that might resemble a direct expression of emotion was one of the signs of this artificiality. Once in reply to a question of mine he said that if he himself had to point out, in his music, passages in which the direct expression of emotion, far from being excluded, had been deliberately attempted, he would begin by selecting the opening of *Asie* in *Shéhérazade* ('la goélette'), then *L'Indifférent* in the same set of songs and, in the *Histoires naturelles, Le Martin-pêcheur,* and the end of *Le Grillon.* He did not mention other obvious instances such as the slow movement of his string Quarter and the *Oiseaux tristes* in *Miroirs.*[1]

Ravel himself, in the Biographical Sketch from which we have quoted so often, cited the following works as being worthy of his own particular affection: *Habanera, Jeux d'eau, Oiseaux tristes, Gaspard de la nuit* and the seventh *Valse noble.* These he considered representative of himself, but it will be noticed that they are among the early works. Roland-Manuel quotes this list in his article preceding the sketch in *La Revue musicale* for December 1938.

Dr. Vaughan Williams, in the letter previously quoted, says that Ravel considered his work 'bien simple toutefois, comme

[1] *Musicians' Gallery* (1933).

Mozart,' which only goes to show that composers know very little about themselves.

Mr. Lennox Berkeley, who knew Ravel well during the time he lived in Paris (1927–33), tells us [1] that Ravel was

very severe on technical matters and detested anything that savoured of improvisation! I think that design in music meant more to him than to most composers—he seemed indifferent if you spoke of any emotion his music caused you, but was delighted if you praised his technical skill. This attitude was very typical; though of a very affectionate nature himself, he hated anything too demonstrative and liked to appear somewhat cold and detached. Though he had many friends, no one seemed able to pass this barrier that he put up, and he was never known to have any intimate relationship with either woman or man, and this is curious when one considers the extreme tenderness and often passionate feeling in his music. Whether it was that his real tastes were in contradiction with his ethical standards, or that he feared any loss of that great self-control and poise, no one will ever know. He was not by any means an ascetic, though; he was fond of good food and wine and smoked very acrid *caporal bleu* cigarettes incessantly.

He would never let anything pass that did not come up to his very strict standard.

Mr. Berkeley also draws attention to his house at Montfort l'Amaury, which he says

might have been made for him; it was full of tiny rooms and in these he had this fantastic collection of *bibelots* and mechanical toys. I remember an object in a little glass case which was a model of a ship at sea—you turned a minute handle and the waves moved and the ship rocked about—he was fascinated by this mixture of ingeniousness and absurdity. And then there was a family of Siamese cats which played a great part in his life.

Compare this, written at the time when Ravel's creative faculties were slowing down, with the statement by M. D. Calvocoressi, who knew him when he was at the top of his form.

At the same time we can think of his remark to Jules Renard

[1] In a letter to the author dated 9th May 1946.

in 1906: 'There is sentimental music, mine, and the intellectual music of d'Indy—they [the followers of d'Indy] do not allow emotion.' [1]

Ravel has always been considered a small master, and this with a certain amount of disparagement. Certainly if we regard a 'master' in the light of vast frescoes and symphonies, we cannot estimate him as in any way comparable with Beethoven, Berlioz, Brahms, Wagner, Elgar or Sibelius. In his own country he could not be considered in the same category as d'Indy, Roussel or Dukas—and for the same reason Debussy must also be excluded from the list of those who can be called great. However, it may be argued that the French *goût* does not run along these lines and that if a composer reflects the characteristics and temper of his own country in a faithful manner, then the substance of his music, provided that the quality is adequate, may credit him with a kind of national greatness.

It has been said that pioneers very often miss greatness because they are unable to crystallize their ideas and bring them to a complete state of fulfilment. The ability to say something new which is worth saying at all is, surely, a proof of greatness—if, indeed, the search for the quality is worth while. It must be remembered that Ravel's most loved works were all written before 1918. *Jeux d'eau* was composed in 1901, the harp Septet in 1906, *Gaspard de la nuit* in 1908 and *Daphnis et Chloé* in 1909 to 1912. What other French music appeared round about that time? Was not Ravel as much ahead of his day as it is possible to imagine? These works are by now established. They said something new, and they still retain their freshness.

By reason of his early works and the influence they brought to bear on the general outlook of French composers of their immediate following, and the stamp imprinted on French music by them, Ravel may truly be said to be a candidate for greatness. The substance of them is rich. Let us admit that if his orchestration is mostly effect and glitter, no one had thought of that particular

[1] *La Revue musicale,* December 1938.

Ravel au
pupitre
« Boléro »

luc. albert moreau

'*La Revue Musicale*'

CONDUCTING 'BOLÉRO'

effect and glitter before him. The harp *glissandi*, the adroit touches on the glockenspiel, the imposing sweeps of violin arpeggios, all these are pure Ravel. They are his hall-mark, his signature, and to decry them must be to decry Ravel himself.

On the piano he brought a romantic imagination to bear as fertile as that of Schumann, and while we may tire of the Sona-tina because every budding pianist has it thrust before him, we can never tire of the sombreness of *Gaspard de la nuit*, the eerie *Le Gibet*, the dazzling *Scarbo*. It may be that the substance of *Miroirs* is not profound, but there is a place in music for exquisite taste and judgment, for the picturesque, for romanticism separated from introspection. Why cannot it be acknowledged that Ravel had greatness in the very slenderness of his textures?

He has suffered at the hands of pianists who see in everything something that is not there. Ravel himself demanded a perfectly cool and even performance of the *Pavane* and the Sonatina; he was driven to fury when he heard pianists romanticizing and sentimentalizing them beyond recognition.

Everything he did he did well. It is all so well organized, so completely apt. The taste is as near perfection as can ever be attained. There are no loose ends or jagged corners. Polish and still more polish. If this element of polish and refinement is the characteristic of the French style and manner, then Ravel is the most consummate artist in music that France has ever produced.

Daphnis et Chloé is a work apart. Ravel himself thought of it as a fresco, a symphony. That it was composed for the theatre makes no difference except that probably he had the vision in front of him of a spectacle which one day would be actuality. If he were incapable of imagining an extended music, of producing thematic breadth and mixing in a sense of colour, no amount of ambitious feelings could have brought this work and all it contains to completion, in the style we have it.

It is no use placing him against such figures as Tchaikovsky or Brahms, Saint-Saëns or d'Indy, and measuring his stature against them. The first two viewed music from an angle of introspection, the second from one of academicism. Only one French composer succeeded in combining tradition with his own national spirit and has formulated a style of his own and of no one else, and that was Albert Roussel. Ravel was not by nature 'symphonic,' but that he could write symphonically when necessary he showed in *Daphnis et Chloé*. Later on he had an outburst of the grand manner—the principal subject of the piano Concerto for the left hand, but this was a flash from which he recoiled.

There is a tendency to concentrate on the *délicieux* aspect of his music. True, the Septet, the Quartet, the Sonatina have this element to a marked degree; and, to a very small extent, *Tzigane*; *La Valse* is decried for its glitter and brilliance—but it was not designed for choreographic purposes and was called, in the first place, *Wien*. This justifies it from all viewpoints. Yet he showed considerable strength in *Le Tombeau de Couperin* and vigour in the *Chansons madécasses*, to say nothing of the exquisite diatonic beauty of the slow movement in the piano Concerto (for both hands). That slow movement is unique in music. It is far too simple to take its place in a Concerto, *per se*, yet completely in keeping with the spirit of the work as a whole. Nothing could be more simple, and nothing more typically *French*.

He suffers, still, from being coupled with Debussy, with whose music his had nothing in common. Debussy waited until the end of his career before he turned to abstract ('cold') music. Ravel produced it at several points in his life, culminating in the two concertos. These concertos have weaknesses as well as good points. It is easy to observe the frivolity and superficiality of the first and last movements of the two-handed piano Concerto (although he wrote thus advisedly) and overlook the tenderness of the slow movement. It is equally easy to note the commonplace jazz effects in the left-hand Concerto, and pass by the dignity, opulence, breadth and nobility of the principal subject. Ravel more than any composer offers loopholes, but his vulnerability is resilient. Every hole can be justified. Each one is Ravel himself, a genius, an artist of the first water, a mind refined and polished to its highest degree.

The music illustrates the man. Surrounded by knick-knacks, both genuine and spurious, dressed faultlessly, brisk and energetic, Ravel *lived*; he did not merely exist. The world was there for his enjoyment, and in return he gave it his genius. He was generous, light-hearted and gregarious where his intimate friends were concerned—and no one ever caught him composing!

Some say that he could never have felt anything deeply because his music and his outward attitude to life were apparent to all comers. He was not one to wear his heart on his sleeve, and he did not consider his innermost feelings of any interest to any one except himself. To his friends he was just 'Ravel,' and his music has a humanity about it with which no basically elusive and aloof composer could ever have endowed it.

Many of those who admire his music may not consider him a great composer; but he was a great French composer—this is undeniable.

APPENDICES

APPENDIX A

CALENDAR

(Figures in brackets denote the age reached by the person mentioned during the year in question)

Year	Age	Life	Contemporary Musicians
1875		Maurice Ravel born March 7, at Ciboure, near Saint-Jean de Luz, Basses-Pyrénées. The family moves to Paris, June.	Bizet (37) dies, June 3; Coleridge-Taylor born, Aug. 15; Montemezzi born, May 31; Roger-Ducasse born, April 18.

Albéniz aged 15; d'Albert 11; Alkan 62; Arensky 14; Balakirev 39; Bantock 8; Boito 33; Bordes 12; Borodin 41; Bossi 14; Brahms 42; Bréville 14; Bruckner 51; Bruneau 18; Busoni 9; Chabrier 34; Charpentier 15; Chausson 20; Cui 40; Delibes 39; Dukas 10; Duparc 27; Dvořák 34; Elgar 18; Fauré 30; Franck 53; Gade 58; Glazunov 10; Goldmark, 45; Gounod 57; Granados 8; Grieg 32; Heller 60; Holst 1; Humperdinck 21; d'Indy 24; Lalo 52; Leoncavallo 17; Liadov 20; Liszt 72; Loeffler 14; MacDowell 14; Mahler 15; Martucci 19;

Year	Age	Life	Contemporary Musicians
			Mascagni 12; Massenet 33; Mussorgsky 36; Novák 5; Offenbach 56; Parry 27; Pedrell 34; Pfitzner 6; Pierné 12; Ponchielli 41; Puccini 17; Raff 53; Rakhmaninov 2; Reger 2; Rimsky-Korsakov 31; Ropartz 11; Roussel 6; Rubinstein 45; Saint-Saëns 40; Satie 9; Schmitt 5; Schoenberg 1; Séverac 2; Sgambati 32; Sibelius 10; Skriabin 3; Smetana 51; Smyth 17; Stanford 23; Strauss (J. ii) 50; Strauss (R.) 11; Suk 1; Sullivan 33; Taneiev 19; Tchaikovsky 35; Thomas (A.) 64; Vaughan Williams, 3; Verdi 62; Wagner 62; Wolf 15.
1876	1		Falla born, Nov. 23; Wolf-Ferrari born, Jan. 12.
1877	2		Dohnányi born, July 27; Holbrooke born, July 5.
1878	3	Birth of brother Édouard	Palmgren born, Feb. 16; Schreker born, March 23.
1879	4		Bridge (Frank) born, Feb. 26; Caplet born, Nov. 27; Delage born, Nov. 13; Grovlez born, April 4; Ireland born, Aug. 13; Medtner born, Dec. 24; Respighi born, July 9; Scott (Cyril) born, Sept. 27.
1880	5		Bloch born, July 24;

Year	Age	Life	Contemporary Musicians
			Inghelbrecht born, Sept. 17; Offenbach (61) dies, Oct. 4; Pizzetti born, Sept. 20.
1881	6		Bartók born, March 25; Miaskovsky born, April 20; Mussorgsky (42) dies, March 28.
1882	7	Begins piano lessons under Henri Ghys.	Kodály born, Dec. 16; Malipiero born, March 18; Raff (60) dies, June 24–5; Stravinsky born, June 17; Turina born, Dec. 9; Vycpálek born, Feb. 23.
1883	8		Bax born, Nov. 6; Casella born, July 25; Szymanowski born, Sept. 21; Wagner (70) dies, Feb. 13; Webern born, Dec. 3; Zandonai born, May 28.
1884	9		van Dieren born, Dec. 27; Griffes born, Sept. 17; Smetana (60) dies, May 12.
1885	10		Berg born, Feb. 7; Wellesz born, Oct. 21.
1886	11	Studies harmony with Charles René.	Kaminski born, July 4; Liszt (75) dies, July 31; Ponchielli (52) dies, Jan. 16.
1887	12		Borodin (53) dies, Feb. 28; Toch born, Dec. 7.
1888	13		Alkan (75) dies, March 29; Durey born, May 27; Heller (74) dies, Jan. 14.
1889	14	Admitted to the preparatory piano class at the Conservatoire. At the Exposition Universelle R. makes his	Shaporin born, Nov. 8.

Year	Age	Life	Contemporary Musicians
		first acquaintance with oriental music.	
1890	15		Franck (68) dies, Nov. 8; Gade (73) dies, Dec. 21; Ibert born, Aug. 15.
1891	16	Enters the piano class of Charles de Bériot (58) at the Conservatoire. Friendship with Ricardo Viñes (16). Studies with Pessard (48) and Dubois (54).	Bliss born, Aug. 2; Delibes (55) dies, Jan. 16; Migot born, Feb. 27; Prokofiev born, April 23; Feb. 27; Roland - Manuel born, March 22.
1892	17		Honegger born, March 10; Jarnach born, July 26; Kilpinen born, Feb. 4; Lalo (69) dies, April 22; Milhaud born, Sept. 4; Tailleferre born, April 19.
1893	18	First composition, *Sérénade grotesque*, for piano	Goossens born, May 26; Gounod (75) dies, Oct. 18; Tchaikovsky (53) dies, Nov. 6.
1894	19	Song, *Ballade de la reine morte*, composed.	Chabrier (53), dies, Sept. 13; Pijper born, Sept. 8; Rubinstein (64) dies, Nov. 20.
1895	20	First published composition, *Menuet antique* for piano. *Habanera* for 2 pianos, No. 1 of *Sites auriculaires*, composed.	Castelnuovo-Tedesco born April 13; Hindemith born. Nov. 16; Sowerby born, May 1.
1896	21	*Entre Cloches* for 2 pianos, the 2nd piece of that set, composed. First published song, *Sainte*.	Bruckner (72) dies, Oct. 11; Sessions born, Dec. 28; Thomas (A.) (85) dies, Feb. 12.

Year	Age	Life	Contemporary Musicians
1897	22		Brahms (64) dies, April 3; Korngold born, May 29.
1898	23	Enters composition class of Fauré (53) at the Conservatoire. Songs, *Deux Épigrammes de Clément Marot*, composed; opera *Schéhérazade* begun. First public performance of a work of his, *Les Sites auriculaires*.	Demuth born, July 15; Rieti born, Jan. 28.
1899	24	The opera dropped, but the overture performed by the Société Nationale, May 27. *Pavane pour un Infante défunte* for piano composed.	Auric born, Feb. 15; Chausson (44) dies, June 10; Poulenc born, Jan. 7; Strauss (J. ii) (74) dies, June 3.
1900	25		Křenek born, Aug. 23; Sullivan (58) dies, Nov. 22.
1901	26	Fails to gain the Prix de Rome, but is awarded the 2nd prize. *Jeux d'eau* for piano composed.	Rubbra born, May 23; Verdi (88) dies, Jan. 27
1902	27	He again fails to take the Prix de Rome. String Quartet begun.	Walton born, March 29.
1903	28	Third failure to take the Prix de Rome. String Quartet finished. Song-cycle *Schérérazade* performed by the Société Nationale.	Wolf (43) dies, Feb. 22.
1904	29		Dvořák (63) dies, May 1.
1905	30	Sonatina and *Miroirs* for piano composed and septet, *Introduction et Allegro*, begun. There is a public scandal when he is not allowed even	Tippett born, Jan. 2.

Year	Age	Life	Contemporary Musicians
		to enter for the Prix de Rome. Visit to Holland.	
1906	31	Song-cycle *Histoires naturelles* composed and performed by the Société Nationale, where it provokes great dissent.	Arensky (45) dies, June 11; Cartan born, Dec. 1; Shostakovitch born, Sept. 25.
1907	32	Opera, *L'Heure espagnole,* and *Rapsodie espagnole* for orchestra composed.	Grieg (64) dies, Sept. 4.
1908	33	*Ma Mère l'Oye* for piano duet and *Gaspard de la nuit* for piano solo composed	MacDowell (47) dies, Jan. 24. Messiaen born Dec. 10. Rimsky-Korsakov (64) dies, June 21.
1909	34	Ballet *Daphnis et Chloé* begun.	Albéniz (49) dies, June 16; Bordes (46) dies, Nov. 18; Martucci (53) dies, June 1.
1910	35	First performance of *Ma Mère l'Oye* at the newly formed Société Musicale Indépendante.	Balakirev (74) dies, May 30.
1911	36	Production of *L'Heure espagnole,* May 19. *Valses nobles et sentimentales* for piano composed and performed anonymously, producing an uproar.	Mahler (51) dies, May 18.
1912	37	*Ma Mère l'Oye* and *Valses nobles* both orchestrated and produced as ballets, the latter as *Adélaïde, ou Le Langage des fleurs* at the Théâtre du Châtelet. *Daphnis et Chloé* finished, produced by Diaghilev's Russian Ballet, June 8.	Coleridge-Taylor (37) dies, Sept. 1; Massenet (70) dies, Aug. 13.

Year	Age	Life	Contemporary Musicians
1913	38	*Trois poèmes de Mallarmé* for voice and chamber music composed. R. collaborates with Stravinsky (31) in orchestrating Mussorgsky's *Khovanshchina*.	Britten born, Nov. 22.
1914	39	Piano Trio composed and *Wien* for orchestra begun. On the outbreak of war R. wishes to join the army, but is rejected. He finally succeeds in joining the Air Force.	Liadov (59) dies, Aug. 28; Sgambati (71) dies, Dec. 15.
1915	40	On active service.	Goldmark (85) dies, Jan. 2; Skriabin (44) dies, April 14; Taneiev (59) dies, June 19.
1916	41	In army hospital.	Granados (49) dies, March 24; Reger (43) dies, May 11.
1917	42	Death of his mother. *Le Tombeau de Couperin* for piano composed, *Wien* turned into the 'choreographic poem' *La Valse* and the opera *L'Enfant et les sortilèges* begun.	
1918	43		Boito (76) dies, June 10; Cui (83) dies, March 14; Debussy (56) dies, March 25; Parry (70) dies, Oct. 7.
1919	44		Leoncavallo (61) dies, Aug. 9.
1920	45	Scandal provoked by his refusal to accept the decoration of the Legion of Honour. *La Valse* performed, Jan. 8, and *Le Tom-*	Bruch (82) dies, Oct. 2; Griffes (36) dies, April 8.

Year	Age	Life	Contemporary Musicians
		beau de Couperin produced as a ballet by the Swedish Ballet. Sonata for violin and cello begun. Visit to Vienna. He buys the villa 'Le Belvédère' at Montfort l'Amaury.	
1921	46		Humperdinck (67) dies, Sept. 27; Saint-Saëns (86) dies, Dec. 16; Séverac (48) dies, March 23.
1922	47	Mussorgsky's *Pictures from an Exhibition* orchestrated and Sonata for violin and cello finished. Visits to Holland, Venice and England.	Pedrell (81) dies, Aug. 19.
1923	48	Violin and piano Sonata begun.	
1924	49	*Tzigane* for violin and piano composed.	Busoni (58) dies, July 27; Fauré (79) dies, Nov. 4; Puccini (66) dies, Nov. 29; Stanford (72) dies, March 29.
1925	50	Production of *L'Enfant et les sortilèges* at Monte Carlo. Carlo. *Chansons madécasses* for voice and chamber music begun.	Satie (59) dies, July 1.
1926	51	*Chansons madécasses* finished.	
1927	52	Violin and piano Sonata finished. Tour in U.S.A.	
1928	53	Return from American tour. *Bolero* for orchestra begun. Visit to England, where he	

Year	Age	Life	Contemporary Musicians
		receives the hon. Mus.D. at Oxford.	
1929	54	Another visit to England.	
1930	55	Two piano concertos (one for left hand) begun.	
1931	56	Both concertos finished. First performances of the left-hand Concerto by Paul Wittgenstein (44), Nov. 27.	d'Indy (80) dies, Dec. 3.
1932	57	European tour during which the G major Concerto is performed at various places by Marguerite Long (58). Commission for a score for a *Don Quixote* film, but he finishes only three songs, *Don Quichotte à Dulcinée*, the rest being given to Ibert (42).	d'Albert (68) dies, March 3; Cartan (26) dies, March 26.
1933	58	First acute signs of brain trouble.	Duparc (85) dies, Feb. 13.
1934	59		Bruneau (77) dies, June 15; Delius (72) dies, June 10; Elgar (77) dies, Feb. 23; Holst (60) dies, May 25.
1935	60	Tour of Spain and North Africa.	Berg (50) dies, Dec. 24; Dukas (70) dies, May 17; Loeffler (75) dies, May 19; Suk (62) dies, May 29.
1936	61	Lives in a distressing mental stupor.	Glazunov (70) dies, March 21; Respighi (56) dies, April 18; van Dieren (52) dies, April 24.
1937	62	Operation decided upon and performed Dec. 10. Ravel dies in Paris, Dec. 28.	Pierné (74) dies, July 17; Roussel (68) dies, Aug. 23; Szymanowski (54) dies, March 29.

Year	Age	Life	Contemporary Musicians
			Auric aged 38; Bantock 69; Bartók 56; Bax 54; Bliss 46; Bloch 57; Bridge (Frank) 58; Britten 24; Casella 54; Castelnuovo - Tedesco 42; Charpentier 77; Demuth 39; Dohnányi 60; Durey 49; Falla 61; Goossens 44; Hindemith 42; Holbrooke 59; Honegger 45; Ireland 58; Jarnach 45; Kaminski 51; Kilpinen 45; Kodály 55; Korngold 40; Křenek 37; Malipiero 55; Mascagni 74; Medtner 58; Messiaen 29; Miaskovsky 56; Milhaud 45; Montemezzi 62; Novák 67; Palmgren 59; Pfitzner 68; Pijper 43; Pizzetti 57; Poulenc 38; Prokofiev 46; Rakhmaninov 64; Rieti 39; Roger-Ducasse 62; Roland-Manuel 46; Ropartz 73; Rubbra 36; Schmitt 67; Schoenberg 63; Schreker 59; Scott (Cyril) 58; Sessions 41; Shaporin 48; Shostakovitch 31; Sibelius 72; Smyth 79; Sowerby 42; Strauss (R.) 73; Stravinsky 55; Tippett 32; Toch 50; Turina 55; Vaughan Williams 65; Vycpálek 55; Walton 35; Webern 54; Wellesz 52; Wolf-Ferrari 61; Zandonai 54.

APPENDIX B

Unpublished Works

SONGS

1894.   *Ballade de la reine morte d'aimer* (Roland de Mares).

1895.   *Un grand sommeil noir* (Verlaine).

1899.   *Si morne* (Verhaeren).

1910.   *Chants populaires* (*Chansons écossaise, flamande, russe*).

PIANO WORKS

1893.   *Sérénade grotesque.*

1895–9.   *Les Sites auriculaires :*
      1. *Habanera.*
      2. *Entre Cloches.*

CANTATAS

1901.   *Myrrha* (F. Boussier).

1902.   *Alcyone* (A. and F. Adonis).

1903.   *Alyssa* (P. Gravollet).

ORCHESTRAL WORKS

1898.   Fairy Overture *Shéhérazade.*

1913.   *Prelude du Fils de l'étoile* (Erik Satie).   Transcription.
    Khovanshchina (Mussorgsky).   Transcription.
    Nocturne, Étude and *Valse* (Chopin).   Transcription.

1914.   *Carnival* (Schumann).   Transcription.

Published Works
SONGS (WITH PIANO)

1896.   *Sainte* (Mallarmé).

Appendix B—Catalogue of Works

1898. *Deux Épigrammes de Clément Marot :*
    1. *D'Anne qui me jecta de la neige.*
    2. *D'Anne jouant de d'espinette.*

1903. *Manteau de fleurs* (P. Gravollet).

1905. *Le Noël des jouets* (M. Ravel).

1906. *Les Grands Vents venus d'outre-mer* (Henri de Régnier).

1906. *Histoires naturelles* (Jules Renard):
    1. *Le Paon.*
    2. *Le Grillon.*
    3. *Le Cygne.*
    4. *Le Martin-pêcheur.*
    5. *La Pintade.*

1907. *Sur l'herbe* (Verlaine).

1907. *Vocalise en forme d'habanera* (wordless).

1907. *Cinq Mélodies populaires grecques* (M. D. Calvocoressi):
    1. *Le Réveil de la mariée.*
    2. *Là-bas vers l'église.*
    3. *Quel galant !*
    4. *Chanson des cueilleuses de lentisques.*
    5. *Tout gai !*

1909. Set II (published 1938).

1910. *Chants populaires :*
    1. *Chanson espagnole.*
    2. *Chanson française.*
    3. *Chanson italienne.*
    4. *Chanson hébraïque.*

1914. *Deux mélodies hébraïques :*
    1. *Kaddisch.*
    2. *L'Énigme éternelle.*

1915. *Trois Chansons* (M. Ravel):
    1. *Nicolette.*
    2. *Trois beaux oiseaux du Paradis*
    3. *Ronde.*
    Originally for mixed chorus.

1924. *Ronsard à son âme* (Ronsard).

1925–6. *Chansons madécasses* (Parny):
    1. *Nahandove.*

2. *Aoua!*
3. *Il est doux.*

1927.   *Rêves* (L. P. Fargue).

1932.   *Don Quichotte à Dulcinée* (P. Morand):
    1. *Chanson romantique.*
    2. *Chanson épique.*
    3. *Chanson à boire.*

PIANO WORKS (SOLO)

1895.   *Menuet antique.*

1899.   *Pavane pour une Infante défunte.*

1901.   *Jeux d'eau.*

1905.   Sonatina.

1905.   *Miroirs:*
    1. *Noctuelles.*
    2. *Oiseaux tristes.*
    3. *Une Barque sur l'océan.*
    4. *Alborada del gracioso.*
    5. *La Vallée des cloches.*

1908.   *Gaspard de la nuit* (after Aloysius Bertrand):
    1. *Ondine.*
    2. *Le Gibet.*
    3. *Scarbo.*

1909.   *Menuet* (on the name 'Haydn').

1911.   *Valses nobles et sentimentales.*

1913.   *Prélude.*

1913.   *À la manière de . . .*
    1. *Borodin.*
    2. *Chabrier.*[1]

1917.   *Le Tombeau de Couperin:*
    1. *Prélude.*
    2. *Fugue.*
    3. *Forlane.*

---

[1] The rest by Alfredo Casella.

    4. *Rigaudon.*
    5. *Menuet.*
    6. *Toccata.*

PIANO WORKS (DUET)

1908.   *Ma Mère l'Oye:*
        1. *Pavane de la Belle au bois dormant.*
        2. *Petit Poucet.*
        3. *Laideronnette, impératrice des pagodes.*
        4. *La Belle et la Bête.*
        5. *Le Jardin féerique.*

1919.   *Frontispice.*

1919–20. *La Valse.*   Transcription.

1927.   *Fanfare* (for *L'Éventail de Jeanne*).

CHAMBER MUSIC

1902–3. String Quartet.

1905–6. Introduction and Allegro (harp, string quartet, flute and clarinet).

1913.   *Trois Poèmes de Stéphane Mallarmé* (voice, piano, string quartet, wo flutes, two clarinets).
        1. *Soupir.*
        2. *Placet futile.*
        3. *Surgi de la croupe et du bond.*

1914.   Trio (piano, violin and cello).

1920–2. Sonata (violin and cello).

1924.   *Tzigane* (violin and piano).

1923–7. Sonata (violin and piano).

1925–6. *Chansons madécasses* (voice, flute, cello and piano).

WORKS FOR ORCHESTRA (ORIGINAL)

1907.   *Rapsodie espagnole:*
        1. *Prélude à la nuit.*
        2. *Malagueña.*
        3. *Habanera.*
        4 *Feria.*

Ravel

WORKS FOR ORCHESTRA (TRANSCRIBED)

1895.   *Menuet antique.*

1899.   *Pavane pour une Infante défunte.*

1905.   *Alborada del gracioso.*

1908.   *Ma Mère l'Oye.*

1911.   *Valses nobles et sentimentales.*

1917.   *Le Tombeau de Couperin* (except *Fugue* and *Toccata*).

WORKS FOR SOLO INSTRUMENT AND ORCHESTRA

1924.   *Tzigane* (violin and orchestra).   Transcription.

1931.   Concerto in D major (piano—left hand—and orchestra).

1931.   Concerto in G major (piano and orchestra).

WORKS FOR VOICE AND ORCHESTRA (ORIGINAL)

1903.   *Shéhérazade* (Tristan Klingsor).
    1. *Asie.*
    2. *La Flûte enchantée.*
    3. *L'Indifférent.*

WORKS FOR VOICE AND ORCHESTRA (TRANSCRIPTIONS)

1903.   *Manteau de fleurs.*

1906.   *Histoires naturelles* (orchestrated by Manuel Rosenthal).

1907.   *Cinq Mélodies populaires grecques:*
    Nos. 1 and 5 orchestrated by Manuel Rosenthal.
    Nos. 2, 3 and 4 orchestrated by Maurice Ravel.

1910.   *Chanson hébraïque.*

1914.   *Deux Mélodies hébraïques.*

1932.   *Don Quichotte à Dulcinée.*

Appendix B—Catalogue of Works

OPERAS

1907.   *L'Heure espagnole* (Franc-Nohain).—'Comédie musicale' in one act.

1920-5. *L'Enfant et les sortilèges* (Colette)—'Fantaisie lyrique' in two parts.

BALLETS

1909-12. *Daphnis et Chloé*.

1912.   *Ma Mère l'Oye* (Prelude and Interludes added).

1919-20. *La Valse* (choreographic poem).

1928.   *Bolero*.

TRANSCRIPTIONS, ORCHESTRATIONS

Debussy: *Prélude à l'Après-midi d'un faune* (two pianos).

Debussy: *Sarabande. Danse.*

Chabrier: *Menuet pompeux.*

Mussorgsky: *Pictures from an Exhibition.*

(The last three orchestrations.)

APPENDIX C

Aranyi, Jelly d' (born 1895), Hungarian violinist, studied with Hubay at Budapest, made her first appearance in Vienna in 1909 and settled in London in 1923.

Aubert, Louis (born 1877), French composer, critic and teacher. Studied at the Paris Conservatoire, lastly under Fauré.

Bathori, Jane (born 1877), French singer. Studied singing and piano in Paris, gave many recitals there and abroad to introduce modern French songs and later went into theatre management in order to produce various new and neglected musical stage works.

Baudelaire, Charles (1821–67), French poet regarded in his time as a decadent, whose *Fleurs du mal* was praised for its beauty and abused for its decadence and immorality.

Bériot, Charles de (1833–1914), French pianist of Belgian descent, son of the famous violinist. Pupil of Thalberg in Paris and later piano professor at the Conservatoire.

Bertrand, Louis (*Aloys*) (1807–42), French poet from whom Ravel had the subject of *Gaspard de la nuit*.

Bordes, Charles (1863–1909), French composer and scholar, pupil of Franck and one of the founders of the Schola Cantorum in Paris.

Bussine, Romain (1830–99), French singer and teacher, professor of singing at the Paris Conservatoire from 1872 and founder, with Saint-Saëns, of the Société Nationale de Musique.

Calvocoressi, M. D. (1877–1944), English critic of Greek descent, educated in France and first active as critic and teacher there, but settled in London from 1914.

Caplet, André (1878–1925), French composer and conductor, influenced by Debussy.

Cœuroy, André (born 1891), French musicologist, pupil of Reger in Germany, later critic in Paris and founder, with Henry Prunières, of the *Revue musicale*.

Colonne, Édouard (1838–1910), French conductor, founder of the orchestra named after him.

Delage, Maurice (born 1879), French composer, pupil of Ravel.

Dubois, Théodore (1837–1924), French organist and composer, took the Prix de Rome in 1861, later became organist at the Madeleine in Paris and from 1896 to 1905 was director of the Conservatoire.

Gédalge, André (1856–1926), French composer, studied at the Paris Conservatoire, where he became professor of counterpoint and fugue in 1905.

Grey, Madeleine (born 1899), French singer, pupil of Hettich for singing and of Cortot for the piano, made her first important appearance in 1921, in Paris.

Guilmant, Alexandre (1837–1911), French organist and composer, studied under his father at Bordeaux and was organist at the Trinité in Paris from 1871 to 1901.

Klingsor, Tristan (*Léon Leclère*) (born 1874), French poet, who adopted two Wagnerian names because he belonged to the school which in the 1890s counted Wagner among its idols.

Koechlin, Charles (born 1867), French composer, studied at the Paris Conservatoire, finally under Fauré. He is a very original and powerful but extremely retiring composer, little known even in France.

Laloy, Louis (1874–1944), French critic and musicologist, studied at the Schola Cantorum in Paris, became lecturer at the Sorbonne in 1906, secretary to the Opéra in 1914 and professor of musical history at the Conservatoire in 1936.

Lenepveu, Charles (1840–1910), French composer. After studying law, he took to music, took the Prix de Rome in 1865, joined the teaching staff of the Conservatoire in 1880 and became professor of composition there in 1894.

Leroux, Xavier (1863–1919), French composer, studied with Massenet and others at the Paris Conservatoire, took the Prix de Rome in 1885 and became professor of harmony at the Conservatoire in 1896.

Long, Marguerite (born 1874), French pianist, studied at the Paris Conservatoire, where she became piano professor in 1920. She married

Joseph de Marliave, author of a book on Beethoven's quartets, and has played and lectured on modern French music in France and abroad.

Mallarmé, Stéphane (1842–98), French poet of the 'decadent' school.

Marnold, Jean (1859–1935), French critic, founder and editor of the *Mercure musical*.

Paladilhe, Émile (1844–1926), French composer, studied at the Paris Conservatoire and gained the Prix de Rome in 1860.

Pessard, Émile (1843–1917), French composer and teacher, studied at the Paris Conservatoire, where he obtained the Prix de Rome in 1866. He became a professor there later.

Reyer, Ernest (1823–1909), French composer, studied privately, became a critic in the 1850s and in 1871 succeeded d'Ortigue as critic of the *Journal des Débats*, which did not prevent him from producing operas and other works.

Rhené-Baton (René Baton) (1879–1940), French conductor and composer, studied at the Paris Conservatoire and after conducting in various provincial towns returned there to become conductor of the Pasdeloup concerts.

Roland-Manuel (born 1891), French composer and critic. Pupil of Roussel at the Schola Cantorum in Paris and of Ravel.

Rolland, Romain (1866–1944), French author and musicologist. He became president of the music section of the École des Hautes Études Sociales in 1901 and later lectured at the Sorbonne and elsewhere. Author of the musical novel *Jean-Christophe* and many books on musical subjects.

Satie, Erik (1866–1925), French composer. He had little systematic musical instruction apart from a year at the Conservatoire, and later played in a café, but he made his mark as a highly original composer and influenced Debussy, Ravel and others. Later became a pupil of Roussel for counterpoint at the Schola Cantorum.

Séverac, Déodat de (1873–1921), French composer, studied at Toulouse and at the Schola Cantorum in Paris, but took no share in official musical life and returned to the south of France, where he quietly devoted himself to composition.

Appendix C—Personalia

Vidal, Paul (1863–1931), French conductor and composer, studied at the Paris Conservatoire, where he took the Prix de Rome in 1883. He became conductor at the Opéra and professor at the Conservatoire.

Viñes, Ricardo (1875–1947), Spanish pianist, studied at Barcelona and Paris, where he lived most of his life, devoting himself to the introduction of piano music by modern composers.

Vuillermoz, Émile (born 1878), French critic and author. After studying law, he went to the Paris Conservatoire, where Fauré was among his masters, and he gave up composition for criticism and musical research.

Wittgenstein, Paul (born 1887), Austrian pianist, pupil of Leschetizky in Vienna. He lost his right arm in the 1914–18 war and devoted himself to the performance and commissioning of piano works for the left hand.

Wolff, Albert (born 1889), French conductor and composer, studied at the Paris Conservatoire, worked at the Opéra-Comique and became by turns conductor of the Lamoureux and Pasdeloup concerts.

APPENDIX D

BIBLIOGRAPHY

Revue musicale, La, Ravel Number (Paris, December 1938).

Colette, Maurice Delage, L. P. Fargue and others, 'Maurice Ravel, par quelques-uns de ses familiers' (Paris, 1939).

Jankélévitch, Vladimir, 'Maurice Ravel' (Paris, 1938).

Roland-Manuel, 'Maurice Ravel et son œuvre' (Paris, 1914).

——, 'Maurice Ravel et son œuvre dramatique' (Paris, 1928).

——, 'A la Gloire de Ravel' (Paris, 1938).

Shera, F. H., 'Debussy and Ravel' (Oxford, 1925).

Séré, Octave, 'Musiciens français d'aujourd'hui' (Paris, 1921).

Chantavoine, Jean, 'De Couperin à Debussy' (Paris, 1920).

Jean-Aubry, G., 'La Musique française d'aujourd'hui' (Paris, 1916).

Tiersot, Julien, 'Un Demi-siècle de musique française: entre les deux guerres' (1870-1917) (Paris, 1917).

APPENDIX E

AEOLIAN HALL

Friday, 19th October 1928, at 8.15

(Under the distinguished patronage of His Excellency the French
Ambassador)

Odette de Foras	*Soprano*	Gwendolen Mason	*Harp*
Frederick Holding	*Violin*	Orrea Pernel	*Second Violin*
Rebecca Clarke	*Viola*	May Mukle	*Cello*
Gordon Bryan	*Piano*	Joseph Slater	*Flute*
	Ralph Clarke	*Clarinet*	

MAURICE RAVEL ⏴ PIANO

Trio in A minor for piano, violin and cello.

Songs:

1. *La Flûte enchantée.*
2. *Tout gai!* (Mélodie populaire grecque).
3. *Deux Épigrammes de Clément Marot.*
4. *Noël des jouets.*
5. *Ronde.*

Accompanied by the Composer.

Introduction and Allegro for harp, with string quartet, flute and clarinet.
Conducted by the Composer.

Toccata from *Le Tombeau de Couperin.*

Chansons madécasses, for voice, flute, cello and piano.
(First performance in England)

Sonata for violin and piano.

Ravel

AEOLIAN HALL

Wednesday, 16th January 1929, at 8.15

(Under the distinguished patronage of His Excellency the French
Ambassador)

Chamber Works and Songs by

DR. MAURICE RAVEL

Artists :

The Composer

Odette de Foras	*Soprano*	Gwendolen Mason	*Harp*
Frederick Holding	*Violin*	Orrea Pernel	*Second Violin*
Rebecca Clarke	*Viola*	May Mukle	*Cello*
Joseph Slater	*Flute*	Arliss Marriott	*Second Flute*
Ralph Clarke	*Clarinet*	George Anderson	*Second Clarinet*

Gordon Bryan   *Piano*

Trio in A minor for piano, violin and cello.

Trois Poèmes de Stéphane Mallarmé.

Sonatina for piano.

Songs:

1. *La Flûte enchantée.*
2. *Sainte.*
3. *D'Anne jouant de l'espinette.*
4. *Air de Conception (L'Heure espagnole).*
5. *Ronsard à son âme.*
6. *Ronde.*

(Accompanied by the Composer)

Introduction and Allegro.

APPENDIX F

ORATION DELIVERED AT OXFORD BY THE PUBLIC ORATOR IN
CONVOCATION,[1] 23RD OCTOBER 1928

CIVEM Francogallicum ad vos duco, patriae suae dulcissimae decus
atque delicias, quem ad mare Cantabricum inter Pyrenaeos nascentem
cum Melpomene placido lumine vidisset, Lutetia, artium nostrarum
mater, excepit modosque musicos numeris legitimis implicare docuit.
Adest vir tenero vegetoque ingenio pollens, cuius ars ab Oriente auspicata
Persiam, Graeciam, Hispaniam illustravit; qui nunc Sanctam et in-
victam Virginem Aurelianam laurea, qua una carebat, donare meditatur.
Artis quidem musicae miracula difficile est Latino sermone illustrare,
neque quisquam oratori veniam denegabit, si nihil dignum pro modorum
illorum inventione ac dispositione dixerit, quos hospes noster vel vocibus
canentium vel digitis psallentium vel pedibus saltantium feliciter est
ausus aptare; si in eo dignos Parrhasio colores, si Pyrgoteleam quandam
in gemmis elimandis sollertiam, strictim tantum attigerit. Quin etiam
ipse veterum fabellarum modulator, qui Materculae suae Anseri cycni
sonum donavit, ignoscet mihi si inter vos argutos absurdius aliquid
strepam; ignoscet si ad Orphea atque Amphiona revolutus tritius eam
artem laudabo, quae non silvas et feras, sed criticos, sed 'horribiles
Britannos' tenet, quae filorum pulsu citra nemorum ruinam per Tempe
campanulis consonantia iam iam, si libebit, nos Academicos audientes
pervehet. Illud autem vir Phoebei praecepti memor non ignoscet, si
nimius ero neque ut ipse materiae parcam, si nihil reticebo aut leni risu
transmittam, si denique Dorconis, non Daphnidis partes agam. Quin
Lesbum hinc facessimus et hoc modulante diem aestivum ibi con-
terimus! Iam Methymnaeorum manibus sacrilegis ereptam Chloen
pastor Daphnis adfatur: iam gaudiorum suorum praeludia, Panis et
Syringis amores saltando in longum ducunt: permittamus illis lepidi
artificis laudes, qui doctis omnibus persuadet Pana non esse mortuum
atque etiam nunc virere Helicona. Itaque missis ambagibus praesento
vobis Musarum interpretem, modorum daedalum, Mauricium Ravel, ut
admittatur ad gradum Doctoris in arte musica honoris causa.

---

[1] Reproduced by kind permission of the Registrar of Oxford University.

INDEX

INDEX

Index

213